BEST & BUZZ WORTHY 2017

WORLD RECORDS, TRENDING TOPICS, AND VIRAL MOMENTS

BY
CYNTHIA O'BRIEN
MICHAEL BRIGHT
DONALD SOMMERVILLE

SCHOLASTIC

Copyright © 2016 by Scholastic Inc.

All rights reserved. Published by Scholastic Inc., *Publishers since 1920*. SCHOLASTIC and associated logos are trademarks and/or registered trademarks of Scholastic Inc.

The publisher does not have any control over and does not assume any responsibility for author or third-party websites or their content.

No part of this publication may be reproduced, stored in a retrieval system, or transmitted in any form or by any means, electronic, mechanical, photocopying, recording, or otherwise, without written permission of the publisher. For information regarding permission, write to Scholastic Inc., Attention: Permissions Department, 557 Broadway, New York, NY 10012.

This book was created and produced by Toucan Books Limited.
Text: Cynthia O'Brien, Michael Bright, Donald Sommerville
Designer: Lee Riches
Editor: Anna Southgate
Editorial Assistant: Autumn Green
Proofreader: Marion Dent
Index: Marie Lorimer
Toucan would like to thank Emily Teresa for picture research.

ISBN 978-1-338-03912-2

10 9 8 7 6 5 4 3 2 1   16 17 18 19 20

Printed in the U.S.A. 40

First printing 2016

contents

music makers
4

1

screen and stage
24

2

on the move
52

3

super structures
76

4

high tech
100

5

amazing animals
126

6

incredible earth
174

7

state stats
208

8

sports stars
262

9

chapter **1**

music makers

Apple takes a bite
New app connects fans and musicians

Apple Music joined the streaming race in 2015, competing with apps such as Spotify. Users of the Apple Music app have access to its Connect feature, which enables direct communication between musicians and fans. Musicians post videos, photographs, and comments, and users can post responses via Messenger, Twitter, Facebook, or email.

MUSIC

THE WORLD'S MUSIC

oy the world's music catalogue.
ring the best of what's new

music trending

Dancing queen
#BeyoncéAlwaysOnBeat

Fans set out to prove that dancing diva Beyoncé can move to any kind of music. They produced hundreds of memes showcasing Queen Bey's talents.

Beyoncé is one of the most popular performers in the world, so it didn't take long for the videos to go viral on Instagram, Twitter, Vine, and YouTube.

Band love

Most retweeted in 2015

In 2015, members of British band One Direction were the talk of Twitter. Harry Styles gathered over 750,000 retweets for his message to bandmate Zayn Malik as news broke that Malik was leaving the group: "All the love as always. H." When Malik congratulated his former group on their new single, he tweeted, "Proud of my boys . . . Big love." Over 570,000 fans retweeted the message.

I'm a Belieber!

Most on-demand streams in one week

Canadian singer Justin Bieber made music history when his album *Purpose* broke Spotify's record for most audio streams in the first week of release. Altogether, the songs from Bieber's platinum-selling album had 205 million streams worldwide, including seventy-seven million in the United States. *Purpose* was released on November 13, 2015.

Hear her roar

Celebrity with the most Twitter followers

More than eighty million people follow Katy Perry's Twitter account. The American singer has tweeted over 6,800 messages since joining the social media site in 2009. Perry has been queen of the Twitter world since overtaking singer Justin Bieber for total number of followers in November 2013. Bieber is in second place with more than seventy-six million followers.

most downloaded song
"uptown funk"

Released in November 2014, "Uptown Funk" spent fourteen weeks at number one on the *Billboard* Hot 100 chart. The retro dance hit by Mark Ronson and featuring Bruno Mars sold over 5.5 million copies—that's over 1 million copies more than the next biggest single, Ed Sheeran's "Thinking Out Loud," also released in 2014. If you think it's always on the radio, you're right: "Uptown Funk" is the most played song of 2015, with 854,000 plays in the United States alone.

Mark Ronson ft. Bruno Mars, "Uptown Funk" 5.52

Most downloaded songs 2015

Units sold in 2015, in millions

Ed Sheeran, "Thinking Out Loud" 3.97

Wiz Khalifa ft. Charlie Puth, "See You Again" 3.80

Adele, "Hello" 3.71

Maroon 5, "Sugar" 3.34

Adele stormed onto the charts with the release of her third album, *25*, on November 20, 2015. By the end of December, the album had become the bestselling album of the year, with 7.44 million copies sold in the United States alone. The album's digital sales totaled $2.3 million, making it the top digital album of the year. Hit songs from the album include "Hello" and "When We Were Young." Adele's previous album, *21*, released in 2011, was the top-selling album of 2011 and 2012, earning $5.82 million the first year and $4.41 million the second.

Top-selling albums 2015

U.S. sales in millions of U.S. dollars

Adele, *25* 7.44

Taylor Swift, *1989* 1.99

Justin Bieber, *Purpose* 1.26

Ed Sheeran, *X* 1.16

Drake, *If You're Reading This It's Too Late* 1.14

most downloaded song in one week

Adele's song "Hello" shot to the top of the charts after its release on October 23, 2015, with over 1.1 million downloads in the United States in just one week. It is the first song ever to reach that total in such a short time. On YouTube, the video for "Hello" had 27.7 million views in twenty-four hours, breaking Taylor Swift's record. "Hello" was released almost a month ahead of the long-awaited 25, Adele's follow-up album to her mega hit 21.

"hello"

top-earning tour 2015

1989

Taylor Swift's 1989 tour earned an incredible $250.4 million in 2015. Starting in Japan in May 2015, the singer played seventy-one shows around the world. Swift's high-energy tour included top hits from her *1989* album, such as "Shake It Off," as well as older favorites, including "I Knew You Were Trouble." Almost 2.3 million fans filled the world's top venues to watch Swift perform multiple dance numbers and sing with surprise guest stars such as The Weeknd, Lorde, and Jason Derulo. A concert movie, *The 1989 World Tour Live*, was released in December 2015.

Top-earning tours of 2015
In millions of U.S. dollars

 Taylor Swift 250.4

AC/DC 180.0

One Direction 158.8

U2 152.8

Foo Fighters 127.0

music makers

drake

first rapper to top billboard 100 chart

Drake released his album *If You're Reading This It's Too Late* through iTunes on February 12, 2015. The digital album sold 495,000 units in its first week and entered the *Billboard* 100 at no. 1, making Drake the first rap artist ever to top the chart. The album also helped Drake secure another record: the most hits on the Billboard 100 at one time.

On March 7, 2015, Drake had fourteen hit songs on the chart, matching the record The Beatles have held since 1964. Since releasing his first hit single, "Best I Ever Had," in 2009, Drake has seen many of his singles go multiplatinum, including "Hotline Bling," which has sold two million copies in the United States as of February 2016.

most watched music video on YouTube 2015

"see you again"

Over 1.6 billion views made "See You Again" the most watched music video in 2015. The song, by Wiz Khalifa featuring Charlie Puth, was uploaded in April and featured on the *Furious 7* soundtrack. "See You Again" topped *Billboard's* Hot 100 chart for twelve weeks. Khalifa's video was a tribute to the actor Paul Walker, who starred in *Furious 7* and the rest of the Fast and Furious franchise. Walker died in November 2013, and his two brothers stepped in to finish his final scenes in the movie. The "See You Again" video ends with the words, "For Paul."

Wiz Khalifa ft. Charlie Puth, "See You Again" 1,166

Most watched music videos

In millions of views

Maroon 5, "Sugar" 872

Ellie Goulding, "Love Me Like You Do" 809

Major Lazer and DJ Snake ft. MØ, "Lean On" 794

Taylor Swift ft. Kendrick Lamar, "Bad Blood" 634

top-selling
recording group
the beatles

Top-selling recording groups in the United States
Albums sold in millions

The Beatles 178

Led Zeppelin 111.5

Eagles 101

Pink Floyd 75

AC/DC 72

The Beatles continue to hold the record for the bestselling recording group in the United States with 178 million albums sold. The British band recorded their first album in September 1962 and made their *Billboard* debut with "I Want to Hold Your Hand." Before breaking up in 1969, the group had twenty number one songs and recorded some of the world's most famous albums, including *Sgt. Pepper's Lonely Hearts Club Band* and *Abbey Road*.

shortest concert ever

In St. John's, Newfoundland, The White Stripes' lead, Jack White, played just one note—a C sharp. The White Stripes had played at least one show in each of Canada's thirteen provinces and territories, as well as "secret" shows in various venues. Die-hard fans found out about these secret shows through posts on The White Stripes messageboard, The Little Room. The one-note show in Newfoundland was a secret event, though hundreds turned up to watch. The official end of the tour was a full set played later that night. *Under Great White Northern Lights*, released in 2010, is a documentary of the tour. The film features backstage moments as well as scenes from the live concerts, and an impromptu performance on a public bus.

the white stripes

top-earning
male singer 2015

Country music star Garth Brooks earned $90 million in 2015, almost $30 million more than top-earning pop star Justin Timberlake. Brooks's album *Man Against Machine*, released in 2014, was the singer's first in thirteen years. Brooks began touring in September 2014, grossing about $1 million per show. Brooks's massively popular blend of country, folk, and stadium rock made country music history when his third album, *Ropin' the Wind*, became the first country album to debut at the top of the pop charts.

garth brooks

Top-earning male singers 2015
In millions of U.S. dollars

Garth Brooks 90

Justin Timberlake 63.5

Ed Sheeran 57

Elton John 53.5

Toby Keith 53

"happy"
by pharrell

Pharrell Williams made history in November 2013 with the release of the first 24-hour music video—the longest music video ever. The video for Williams's hit song "Happy" is a four-minute track that plays on a loop 360 times. In addition to Williams, celebrities such as Jamie Foxx, Steve Carell, and Miranda Cosgrove make appearances in the video. In 2014, "Happy" broke records again, becoming the first single to top six *Billboard* charts in one year and becoming the year's bestselling song with 6,455,000 digital copies sold.

top-earning
female
singer
2015

katy perry

Katy Perry raked in $135 million in 2015, mostly from her seventeen-month Prismatic World Tour that started in Ireland and ended in Costa Rica. The tour consisted of 151 concerts across the globe. Songs in Perry's set included her hit "Roar" from her album *Prism*, released in 2013, along with previous hits, such as "Teenage Dream," "California Gurls," and "Firework." *Katy Perry: The Prismatic World Tour* movie was released in March 2015.

Top-earning female singers 2015

In millions of U.S. dollars

Katy Perry **135**

Taylor Swift **80**

Lady Gaga **59**

Beyoncé **54.5**

Britney Spears **31**

digital artist

rihanna

Top-selling digital artists in the United States

In millions

Rihanna is the first singer to sell more than 100 million digital singles—that's more than any artist in history. The Recording Industry Association of America (RIAA) awards gold certificates for 500,000 copies sold and platinum for one million sold. Of Rihanna's fifty-eight singles, "We Found Love" has the most certifications with nine platinums. Three other songs, "Stay," "What's My Name," and "Only Girl (in the World)," have six platinum certifications each. Rihanna's first hit, "Pon de Replay," was number two on the *Billboard* singles chart in 2005, and she continued to top the charts with "SOS," "Disturbia," and many more.

Rihanna **102**

Taylor Swift **96.5**

Katy Perry **83.5**

Kanye West **48**

Lady Gaga **40.5**

bestselling digital song of all time

"baby"

Justin Bieber's hit single "Baby" has sold twelve million copies since its release in March 2010. "Baby," featuring rapper Ludacris, appeared on Bieber's debut studio album, *My World*, which was nominated for a Grammy Award in 2011. Bieber began his career singing in videos on YouTube before he was discovered by a talent agent and offered a recording contract. His first single, "One Time," went platinum in January 2010, having sold one million copies since its release in June 2009. Bieber's latest album, *Purpose*, went platinum just three weeks after its release.

Bestselling digital songs in the United States

In millions

Justin Bieber, ft. Ludacris, "Baby" 12

Eminem, ft. Rihanna, "Love the Way You Lie" 11

Lady Gaga, "Bad Romance" 11

Imagine Dragons, "Radioactive" 10

Katy Perry, "Dark Horse" 10

musician with the most MTV video music awards

Madonna is the queen of the MTV Video Music Awards, having scooped up twenty awards in all. The singer won her first MTV honor, the Video Vanguard Award, in 1986—just two years after the ceremony started. She won Best Female Video a year later for "Papa Don't Preach." Other award-winning videos include "Express Yourself," "Vogue," and "Beautiful Stranger." Madonna's "Ray of Light" video earned the most, picking up six awards altogether, including Best Female Video and Video of the Year.

madonna

Musicians with the most MTV Video Music Awards

Madonna 20

Beyoncé 16

Lady Gaga 13

Peter Gabriel 13

Eminem 12

george strait

act with the most country music awards

"King of Country" George Strait won his first Country Music Awards (CMA) in 1985 for Male Vocalist of the Year and Album of the Year. Since then, Strait has won an amazing twenty-two CMAs, including Entertainer of the Year in 2013. The country music superstar has thirty-three platinum or multiplatinum albums, and he holds the record for the most platinum certifications in country music. George Strait was inducted into the Country Music Hall of Fame in 2006.

bestselling digital country music artist

Award-winning country singer Carrie Underwood has sold twenty-nine million digital singles, making her the top-selling country artist. She has won Female Vocalist of the Year six times—three each from the Country Music Association (CMA) and the Academy of Country Music (ACM)—and five Grammy Awards. Underwood's biggest hits include "Before He Cheats," which was the first country song to sell over two million copies digitally, and "Jesus, Take The Wheel," which has sold three million copies. She released her first album, *Some Hearts*, in November 2005 after winning season four of *American Idol*, and her fifth studio album, *Storyteller*, was released in October 2015.

carrie underwood

Carrie Underwood **29**

Jason Aldean **26**

Florida Georgia Line **23**

Blake Shelton **22**

Tim McGraw **17.5**

Bestselling digital country music artists
Millions of units sold

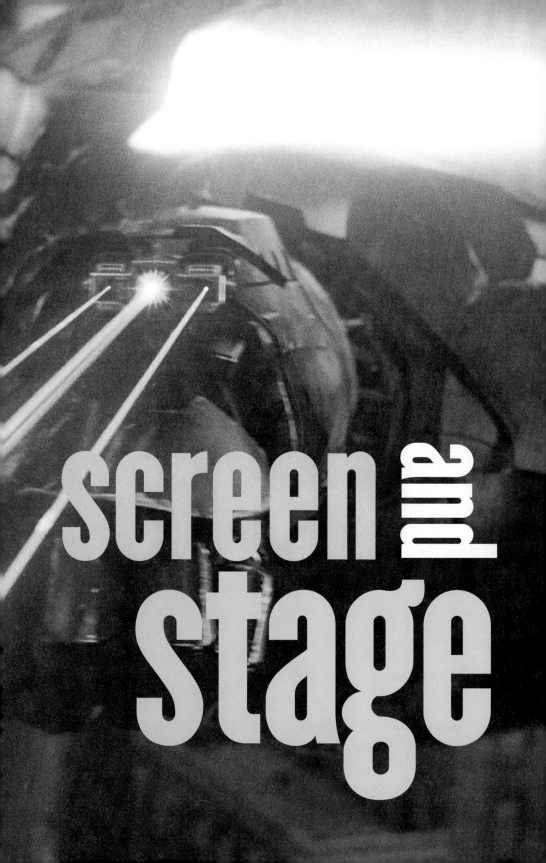

screen and stage

Kanye for president!

Most tweeted TV minute

In 2015's most tweeted TV minute, Kanye West came out on top with 248,000 tweets at 10:49 p.m. during the *MTV Video Music Awards* on August 30. The rush of tweets came in response to West's announcement that he would run for president in 2020.

trending

movies television theater

Rock On

Fastest Broadway video to reach one million views online

When Andrew Lloyd Webber released a 360-degree view of his *School of Rock* stage production, the video reached one million views on Facebook and YouTube in less than three days. The video featured the song "You're in the Band" and allowed viewers to use the new 360-degree technology to zoom around the real-life classroom setting.

Teenage streams

Most popular streaming service

Netflix was the top on-demand video service in 2015, beating out competitors such as Amazon and Hulu. By the end of 2015, Netflix had 74.7 million subscribers. The biggest change in viewing is among younger viewers, who watch four times more online content than older viewers. Almost 80 percent of people aged eighteen to thirty-four used streaming services in 2015.

Tiny dancer

Reality TV performer hits YouTube billion

Maddie Ziegler first made herself known on the reality show *Dance Moms*, but the young dancer became a worldwide phenomenon when she showed off her skills in three of singer Sia's music videos. The videos gained over 1.1 billion views in 2015. Zeigler's popularity also soared on Instagram with over five million followers.

Disney princess

Most reblogged actress

American actress, singer, and dancer Zendaya was Tumblr's most reblogged actress in 2015. The Disney Channel star played Rocky Blue in *Shake It Up*, and in 2015, she landed the lead role in Disney's *K.C. Undercover*. In May 2015, Zendaya showed a darker side as the character Cut-Throat in Taylor Swift's hit video for *Bad Blood*.

longest-running
scripted TV show in
the united states
the simpsons

In 2015, *The Simpsons* celebrated its twenty-seventh season, making the show the longest-running American sitcom, cartoon, and scripted prime-time television show in history. The animated comedy, which first aired in December 1989, centers on the antics and everyday lives of the Simpson family. The show's creator, Matt Groening, named the characters after members in his own family, although he substituted Bart for his own name. Recent guest stars include Adam Driver and Kristen Bell.

MATT GROENING

TV show with the most emmy awards

The variety show *Saturday Night Live* has won forty-two Emmy Awards since it premiered in 1975. The late-night comedy show broadcasts live from New York City's Rockefeller Center on Saturday nights. *Saturday Night Live* launched the careers of America's top comedians, including Will Ferrell, Tina Fey, Chris Rock, and Adam Sandler, many of whom return to the show regularly in guest spots. A new celebrity host introduces the show each week and takes part in the comedy skits with the regular cast. Musical guests in 2015 included The Weeknd, Miley Cyrus, and Rihanna.

SATURDAY NIGHT LIVE

highest-paid TV actresses
sofía vergara
and
kaley cuoco

Modern Family's Sofía Vergara and Kaley Cuoco from *The Big Bang Theory* each earned $28.5 million in 2015. Both TV shows are hit comedies with numerous awards between them. Vergara, originally from Colombia, has won four Screen Actors Guild Awards as part of the *Modern Family* cast for Outstanding Performance by an Ensemble in a Comedy Series. American actress Cuoco started acting at six years old and won acclaim for her role in *8 Simple Rules*. In 2015, she won the People's Choice Award for Favorite Comedic TV Actress.

Sofía Vergara 28.5

Kaley Cuoco 28.5

Top-earning TV actresses

In millions of U.S. dollars

Julie Bowen 12

Ellen Pompeo 11.5

Mariska Hargitay 11

celebrity with the most
kids' choice awards
will smith

Will Smith has won 10 Kids' Choice Awards, including two Best Actor wins for his roles in *The Fresh Prince of Bel-Air* and *Hancock*. Will Smith's career took off with *The Fresh Prince of Bel-Air*, a sitcom that aired for six years in the 1990s. He went on to have a highly successful movie career, earning two Academy Award nominations for *The Pursuit of Happyness* and *Ali*. Nickelodeon introduced the Kids' Choice Awards in 1988—a highlight of the show is its tradition of "sliming" celebrity guests with green goo, often taking them by surprise.

Will Smith 10

Adam Sandler 9

Selena Gomez 8

Miley Cyrus 7

Amanda Bynes 7

Celebrities with the most Kids' Choice Awards

most popular tv show

NBC sunday night football

More than 23 million fans tune in every week for *NBC Sunday Night Football*, making the sports program the top-rated show in the United States in 2015. *NFL Thursday Night Football* is not far behind, with an average of 17.5 million viewers each week. *NBC Sunday Night Football* has won numerous Sports Emmy Awards since its first show in 2006. Hosts include Cris Collinsworth, a top sports analyst, Al Michaels, the play-by-play commentator, and Michele Tafoya, the sideline reporter.

highest-paid
tv actor

Jim Parsons earned $29 million in 2015 playing television's favorite physicist, Sheldon Cooper, in *The Big Bang Theory*. His costars Johnny Galecki, Simon Helberg, and Kunal Nayyar also made the list of the highest-earning actors. Both Parsons and Galecki signed new contracts in 2015, increasing their pay to $1 million per episode. Parsons appeared in numerous TV shows before getting his big break in 2006 with a lead role as Sheldon. He has since won four Emmy Awards for Outstanding Lead Actor in a Comedy Series.

jim parsons

Highest-paid TV actors
In millions of U.S. dollars

Jim Parsons	29
Johnny Galecki	27
Mark Harmon	20
Simon Helberg	20
Kunal Nayyar	20

PIRATES OF THE CARIBBEAN ON STRANGER TIDES

Pirates of the Caribbean: On Stranger Tides cost a huge $378.5 million to produce, almost $80 million more than *Pirates of the Caribbean: At World's End*, released four years earlier. The 2011 movie was the fourth in Walt Disney's Pirates of the Caribbean franchise starring Johnny Depp as Captain Jack Sparrow. In this installment of the wildly popular series, Captain Jack goes in search of the Fountain of Youth. Depp earned $55.5 million for the role, and the movie went on to earn $1.04 billion worldwide. Johnny Depp returns to play Captain Jack in *Pirates of the Caribbean: Dead Men Tell No Tales*, due for release in 2017.

Movies with the highest production costs
In millions of U.S. dollars

Pirates of the Caribbean: On Stranger Tides **378.5**

Pirates of the Caribbean: At World's End **300.0**

movie with the highest production costs

Avengers: Age of Ultron **279.9**

John Carter **263.7**

Tangled **260.0**

most successful movie franchise
marvel cinematic universe

The Marvel Comics superhero movie franchise has grossed over $9 billion worldwide—and counting! *The Avengers*, released in 2012, is the top-grossing movie in the Marvel Cinematic Universe, having earned $1.52 billion worldwide. The movie features Marvel's best-loved superheroes, including Iron Man, played by Robert Downey Jr., and Captain America, played by Chris Evans. The Marvel franchise also includes blockbuster movies starring individual superheroes such as *Iron Man*, *Thor*, *Ant-Man*, *Captain America*, and *The Incredible Hulk*.

$ $ $ $ $ **Marvel Cinematic Universe 9. 08**

$ $ $ $ **Harry Potter 7.72**

$ $ $ **James Bond 6.98**

Tolkien's Middle-Earth 5.88

$ **Star Wars 4.92**

Most successful movie franchises

Total worldwide gross, in billions of U.S. dollars

movies with the most oscars

Movies with the most Oscars

Ben-Hur (1959) 11

Titanic (1997) 11

The Lord of the Rings: The Return of the King (2003) 11

West Side Story (1961) 10

The Last Emperor (1987) 9

It's a three-way tie for the movie with the most Academy Awards: *Ben-Hur*, *Titanic*, and *The Lord of the Rings: The Return of the King* have each won eleven Oscars, including Best Picture and Best Director. The 1959 biblical epic *Ben-Hur* was the first to achieve the record number of wins. *Titanic*, based on the real 1912 disaster, won numerous Oscars for its striking visual and sound effects. *The Lord of the Rings: The Return of the King* was the third in a trilogy based on the books by J. R. R. Tolkien. It is the only movie of the top three to win in every category in which it was nominated.

So who's Oscar?

Every year the Academy of Motion Picture Arts and Sciences presents awards in recognition of the greatest achievements in the film industry. Those actors, directors, screenplay writers, and producers lucky enough to win each receive a highly prized golden statuette A.K.A. Oscar. No one really knows where the name comes from, although it is thought to have originated among the Hollywood greats of the 1930s—Bette Davis and Walt Disney have been credited, among others. Either way, Oscar became the official nickname for the Academy Award in 1939.

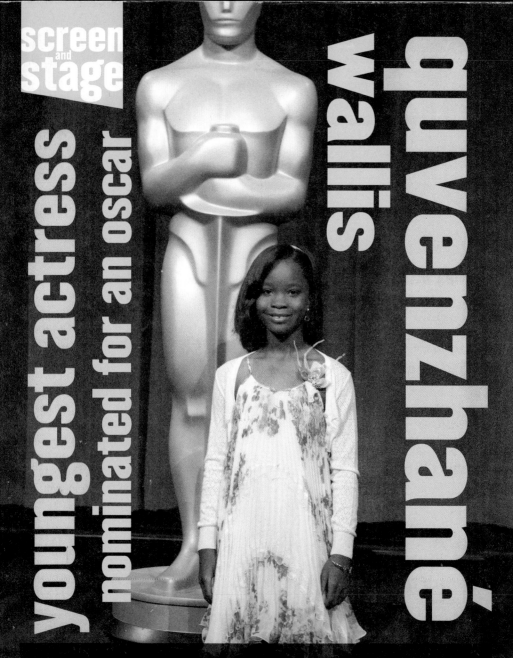

quvenzhané wallis

youngest actress
nominated for an oscar

At nine years old, Quvenzhané Wallis became the youngest-ever Academy Award nominee. The actress received the Best Actress nomination in 2012 for her role as Hushpuppy in *Beasts of the Southern Wild*. Although Wallis did not win the Oscar, she went on to gain thirty-nine more nominations and win twenty-two awards at various industry award shows. In 2015, she received a Golden Globe Best Actress nomination for her role in *Annie*. Wallis was five years old when she auditioned for Hushpuppy (the minimum age was six), and she won the part over four thousand other candidates.

Justin Henry was just seven years old when he received a Best Supporting Actor nomination for *Kramer vs. Kramer* in 1979. His neighbor, a casting director, suggested that Henry try out for the part. Although the young actor lost out on the Oscar, *Kramer vs. Kramer* won several Oscars, including Best Actor for Dustin Hoffman, Best Actress in a Supporting Role for Meryl Streep, and Best Picture. Justin Henry appeared in a few other films before leaving acting to finish his education. He then returned to acting in the 1990s.

justin henry

youngest actor
nominated for an oscar

Movies with the most successful domestic opening weekend

Weekend earnings, in millions of U.S. dollars

Star Wars: The Force Awakens (12/18/15) 247.9

Jurassic World (6/12/15) 208.8

Marvel's The Avengers (5/4/12) 207.4

Avengers: Age of Ultron (5/1/15) 191.2

Iron Man 3 (5/3/13) 174.1

Star Wars: Episode VII: The Force Awakens broke box-office records in December 2015 as the movie with the most successful opening weekend in the United States and the movie that earned the most money in a single day. The hugely anticipated movie opened on December 18, 2015, around the world (everywhere but China, where it premiered January 9, 2016). The movie's opening weekend earned an incredible $247,966,675 in the United States and $528,966,675 worldwide. The film broke another record when it took just twelve days to reach $1 billion worldwide, faster than any film in history. On its opening day alone, *Star Wars: The Force Awakens* earned over $119 million.

STAR WARS: EPISODE VII: THE FORCE AWAKENS

smashes box office records!

Original cast members Harrison Ford, Carrie Fisher, and Mark Hamill joined new stars Daisy Ridley, John Boyega, and Oscar Isaac. Directed by J. J. Abrams, *Star Wars: The Force Awakens* opened ten years after the release of the last film in the franchise, *Star Wars: Episode III: Revenge of the Sith*. Two more sequels are planned for release in the coming years.

Kristen Stewart

actress with the most
MTV movie awards

Twilight actress Kristen Stewart has won seven MTV Movie Awards for her role as Bella Swan in the vampire movie saga. The movies are film adaptations of Stephenie Meyer's bestselling books. Stewart won four of the awards for Best Kiss with her costar, Robert Pattinson. The other three awards were for Best Female Performance in *Twilight* (2008), *The Twilight Saga: New Moon* (2009), and *The Twilight Saga: Eclipse* (2010).

Actresses with the most MTV Movie Awards

⭐⭐⭐⭐⭐ **Kristen Stewart 7**

⭐⭐⭐⭐ **Jennifer Lawrence 5**   ⭐⭐⭐ **Alicia Silverstone 4**

⭐⭐⭐ **Sandra Bullock 4**   ⭐⭐⭐ **Shailene Woodley 4**

actor with the most MTV movie awards

jim carrey

Jim Carrey has eleven MTV Movie Awards, including five Best Comedic Performance awards for his roles in *Dumb and Dumber* (1994), *Ace Ventura: When Nature Calls* (1995), *The Cable Guy* (1996), *Liar Liar* (1997), and *Yes Man* (2008). He won the Best Villain award twice, once for Dr. Seuss' *How the Grinch Stole Christmas* (2000) and the second time for *The Cable Guy*. Fans also awarded Carrey with the Best Kiss award for his lip-lock with Lauren Holly in *Dumb and Dumber*.

Actors with the most MTV Movie Awards

★★★★★ Jim Carrey 11

★★★★ Robert Pattinson 10

★★★ Mike Myers 7

★★ Adam Sandler 6

★ Johnny Depp 5

top-earning
actress
jennifer

lawrence

Jennifer Lawrence earned a colossal $52 million in 2015. The actress, who plays Katniss Everdeen in the smash-hit series The Hunger Games, took home $7.5 million apiece for *Mockingjay: Parts 1* and *2*. She negotiated an even bigger salary for *Joy* (December 2015), earning $15 million for her leading role. In 2015, Lawrence made headlines with an essay on how male actors frequently get paid more than female actors for similar roles.

Top-earning actresses
In millions of U.S. dollars

Jennifer Lawrence 52

Scarlett Johansson 35.5

Melissa McCarthy 23

Bingbing Fan 21

Jennifer Aniston 16.5

top-earning actor robert downey jr.

Robert Downey Jr. earned $80 million in 2015, making him the top-earning actor for the third year in a row. In 2015, Downey Jr. reprised his role as Iron Man in *Avengers: Age of Ultron*, the sequel to 2012's huge hit *The Avengers*. In addition, Downey Jr. has starred as the superhero in three Iron Man movies. *Avengers: Age of Ultron* grossed over $1.4 billion worldwide, the third top-grossing movie of 2015 in the United States.

Top-earning actors
In millions of U.S. dollars

Robert Downey Jr. 80

Jackie Chan 50

Vin Diesel 47

Bradley Cooper 41.5

Adam Sandler 41

jurassic world

top-grossing movie of 2015

🍿🍿🍿🍿🍿 *Jurassic World* 1.66

🍿🍿🍿🍿 *Star Wars: The Force Awakens* 1.60

🍿🍿🍿 *Furious 7* 1.51

🍿🍿 *Avengers: Age of Ultron* 1.40

🍿 *Minions* 1.15

Top-grossing movies 2015

Worldwide gross in billions of U.S. dollars

Jurassic World opened June 12, 2015, grossing over $650 million in the United States and over $1.6 billion worldwide. The movie's opening weekend grossed $208 million in the United States, the second-highest-ranking movie in history after *Star Wars: The Force Awakens*.

The dinosaur epic starred Chris Pratt and Bryce Dallas Howard and is the fourth movie in the Jurassic Park series. The *Jurassic World* plot focuses on a dinosaur theme park that becomes a high-danger zone when a genetically modified dinosaur escapes.

frozen

Disney's *Frozen*, which opened in November 2013, is the top-grossing animated movie worldwide, earning over $1 billion since its release. It is eighth on the list of the ten highest-grossing movies of all time. At the Oscars in February 2014, the film won Academy Awards for Best Animated Feature and Best Original Song. *Frozen* tells the story of two sisters: Elsa, voiced by Idina Menzel, and Anna, voiced by Kristen Bell. Its hit song, "Let it Go," won the Oscar for Best Original Song in 2014 and has sold over eight million digital copies in the United States alone.

Frozen 1.27 billion

Minions 1.15 billion

Toy Story 3 1.06 billion

**The Lion King
987.5 million**

**Despicable Me 2
970.8 million**

**Top-grossing
animated movies**

Worldwide gross in
U.S. dollars

Andrew Lloyd Webber's *The Phantom of the Opera* opened on Broadway in January 1988 and has been performed more than 11,600 times. The original London cast members, Michael Crawford, Sarah Brightman, and Steve Barton, reprised their roles on Broadway. The story, based on a novel written in 1911 by French author Gaston Leroux, tells the tragic tale of the phantom and his love for an opera singer, Christine.

longest-running broadway show

the phantom of the opera

Longest-running Broadway shows
Total performances (as of January 2016)

🎭🎭🎭🎭🎭 **The Phantom of the Opera 11,629**

🎭🎭🎭 *Chicago (1996 Revival)* **7,952**   🎭🎭🎭 *The Lion King* **7,563**

🎭🎭 *Cats* **7,485**   🎭 *Les Misérables* **6,680**

highest-grossing
broadway
musical
the lion king

Since opening on November 13, 1997, *The Lion King* has earned $1.2 billion. The show is Broadway's third-longest-running production. *The Lion King* stage show is an adaptation of the hugely popular Disney animated film. Along with hit songs from the movie such as "Circle of Life" and "Hakuna Matata," the show includes new compositions by South African composer Lebo M. and others. The Broadway show features songs in six African languages, including Swahili and Congolese. Since it opened, *The Lion King* has attracted audiences totaling over eighty million people.

musical with the most tony awards

the producers

The Producers opened on Broadway in April 2001. At that year's Tony Awards, the musical was nominated for fifteen awards and went on to win a record twelve Tonys, including Best Musical, Original Score, Choreography, Costume Design, and Actor in a Musical. The smash hit continued to run for a total of 2,502 performances before closing in April 2007, grossing over $288 million altogether.

youngest winner
of a
laurence olivier award

In 2012, four actresses shared an Olivier Award for their roles in the British production of *Matilda*. Eleanor Worthington-Cox, Cleo Demetriou, Kerry Ingram, and Sophia Kiely all won the award for Best Actress in a Musical. Of the four actresses, Worthington-Cox, age ten, was youngest by a few weeks. Each actress portraying Matilda performs two shows a week. In the U.S., the four *Matilda* actresses won a special Tony Honors for Excellence in the Theater in 2013. *Matilda*, inspired by the book by Roald Dahl, won a record seven Olivier Awards in 2012.

cleo demetriou

eleanor worthington-cox

kerry ingram

sophia kiely

chapter **3**

Life on Mars?

#MarsWater

Scientists finally had their suspicions confirmed in September 2015: There is water on Mars. Twitter lit up with the news when the latest discovery from NASA's Mars Reconnaissance Orbiter (MRO) was announced. The spacecraft detected water in certain areas of the planet that seems to flow in higher temperatures (above −10 degrees Fahrenheit).

trending
on the
move

Pluto gets a close-up

Closest images of distant dwarf planet

NASA's *New Horizons* spacecraft passed within 7,800 miles of Pluto in July 2015. It took nine years for *New Horizons* to reach the faraway dwarf planet, and for the first time, scientists will have access to amazing information about the outer reaches of our solar system. Just before its flyby, *New Horizons* sent photos to Earth—a distance of 476,000 miles—and prompted dozens of memes.

On the fast track

Race car driver with the most Twitter followers

Race car driver Danica Patrick is a social media favorite and her followers prove it—she has over 1.4 million followers on Twitter and over 1.4 million "likes" on her Facebook page. Since becoming the first woman to lead laps and finish in the top five at the Indy 500 in 2005, Patrick has continued to break records on and off the track. She has appeared in thirteen Super Bowl ads—more than any other celebrity.

Cruise control

Most social media usage at sea

When the *Norwegian Escape* cruise ship launched in October 2015, people took to social media in record numbers. During its inaugural celebrations, the ship prompted over 576,000 Facebook posts, 11,000 Instagram photos, and 14,000 tweets including the tag #norwegianescape. The ship is the fifth-largest cruise ship in the world.

Precision guidance

Most expensive selfie

Google searches for "Rosetta selfie" rocketed after the European Space Agency's *Rosetta* spacecraft snapped a selfie showing the side of the craft and its solar wings with comet 67P/Churyumov-Gerasimenko just ten miles away in the background. It took a decade for *Rosetta* to reach the comet, and just seven hours for it to drop onto the surface of the tiny space body. *Rosetta* sent back valuable data on the chemical composition of the comet, showing that water-rich comets were not the source of Earth's water, as was once thought.

comet 67P

solar wings

world's first monster school bus

"Bad to the Bone" is the first monster school bus in the world. This revamped 1956 yellow bus is 13 feet high, thanks to massive tires with 25-inch rims. The oversized bus weighs 19,000 pounds and is a favorite ride at charity events in California. But don't expect to get anywhere in a hurry—this "Kool Bus" is not built for speed and goes at a maximum of just 7 miles per hour.

most expensive street-legal car
koenigsegg CCXR trevita

The world's most expensive car ever—a Koenigsegg CCXR Trevita—sold for $4.8 million in 2015. At top speed, the hypercar can hit 254 miles per hour. Koenigsegg, a Swedish manufacturer, built just two Trevitas. One of the vehicle's unique features is the specially created white carbon fiber body, which also gives the car its name: Trevita means "three whites" in Swedish. On its website, Koenigsegg boasts that the Trevita "shines like millions of diamonds" in the sun.

Most expensive cars
(for 2015) In U.S. dollars

$$$$$ Koenigsegg CCXR Trevita $4.8 million

$$$$ Lamborghini Veneno $4.5 million

$$$ Mansory Vivere Bugatti Veyron $3.5 million

$$$ W Motors Lykan Hypersport $3.4 million

$$$ Ferrari F60 America $2.5 million

57

biggest monster truck

bigfoot

Standing 15 feet 6 inches tall and weighing 38,000 pounds, Bigfoot #5 is the king of monster trucks. Bob Chandler purchased a Ford pickup truck in 1974 and began creating the first Bigfoot monster truck in 1975. In 1986, Chandler introduced Bigfoot #5, the largest ever. The truck's tires are 10 feet tall and come from an Alaskan land train used by the U.S. Army in the 1950s. Chandler built over a dozen more Bigfoot trucks, but none of these newbies matches the size of Bigfoot #5.

QTvan

smallest trailer

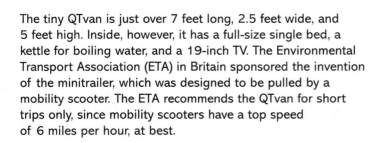

The tiny QTvan is just over 7 feet long, 2.5 feet wide, and 5 feet high. Inside, however, it has a full-size single bed, a kettle for boiling water, and a 19-inch TV. The Environmental Transport Association (ETA) in Britain sponsored the invention of the minitrailer, which was designed to be pulled by a mobility scooter. The ETA recommends the QTvan for short trips only, since mobility scooters have a top speed of 6 miles per hour, at best.

fastest land vehicle

thrust

thrust SSC

The world's fastest car is the Thrust SSC, which reached a speed of 763 miles per hour on October 15, 1997, in the Black Rock Desert, Nevada. SSC stands for supersonic (faster than the speed of sound). The Thrust SSC's amazing speed comes from two jet engines with 110,000 brake horsepower. That's as much as 145 Formula One race cars. The British-made car uses about 5 gallons of jet fuel in one second and takes just five seconds to reach its top speed. At that speed, the Thrust SSC could travel from New York City to San Francisco in less than four hours. More recently, another British manufacturer has developed a new supersonic car, the Bloodhound, with a projected speed of 1,000 miles per hour. If it reaches that, it will set a new world record.

fastest passenger
train maglev

In April 2015, a Japanese seven-car Maglev train hit a top speed of 375 miles per hour on a test track near Mount Fuji. Maglev trains hover about 4 inches over the tracks. Electrically charged magnets propel the train forward, and it is the lack of friction that enables the train to go at such astonishing speeds. A new track under construction will carry the train 178 miles between Tokyo, Nagoya, and Osaka, cutting travel time by 50 percent. Central Japan Railway expects the train's operational speed to be a maximum of 314 miles per hour.

Fastest passenger trains

Japan Maglev train 375 mph

China CRH380AL 302 mph

Germany TR-09 279 mph

Japan Shinkansen bullet train 275 mph

Shanghai Maglev 268 mph

fastest street-legal motorcycle

madmax streetfighter

The Madmax Streetfighter is the world's fastest street-legal motorcycle with a top speed of 233 miles per hour. A lightweight, high-performance engine with over 500 brake horsepower enables the bike to cover 340 feet per second at full throttle. Maxicorp Autosports Madmax Race Team used the MTT Y2K Turbine Superbike as a basis for its new bike. They made engine parts using strong, but light, titanium and reduced the two-speed gearbox to a single-speed gearbox. However, the Madmax Streetfighter may not be for everyone. It costs over $300,000 to build, and its creators believe it is too powerful for most riders.

first highway
automatic steering

tesla autopilot

Self-driving cars became closer to a reality in 2015 when Tesla launched Autopilot. The software upgrade for their cars allows automatic parking, hands-free lane changes, and automatic lane control, in addition to cruise control. Another feature, called Summon, allows drivers to use an app to tell their cars to open the garage door and drive outside to wait for them.

fastest helicopter

In June 2013, the Eurocopter X3 reached 302 miles per hour during a descent, smashing all previous helicopter speed records. At level flight, the helicopter reached a speed of 293 miles per hour, also breaking the previous world record of 287 miles per hour, held by the Sikorsky X2 since 2010.

Eurocopter, now Airbus Helicopter, built the high-speed aircraft as a technology demonstrator. Two Rolls-Royce Turbomeca RTM322 engines powered the X3's five-blade main rotor and its two tractor propellers. Today, the record-breaking helicopter is on display at the Air and Space Museum in France.

eurocopter X3

Fastest helicopters

Maximum speed in miles per hour

Eurocopter X3
302 mph

Sikorsky X2
287 mph

Bell Boeing V-22 Osprey 275 mph

G-LYNX
249 mph

Sikorsky S-76
177 mph

lightest jet

BD-5J microjet

In 2004, the BD-5J Microjet, a one-seater aircraft, secured the record as the world's lightest jet. The jet weighs 358.8 pounds, has a 17-foot wingspan, and is just 12 feet long. Engineer Jim Bede introduced the microjet in the early 1970s and sold hundreds in kit form, ready for self-assembly. The BD-5J model became a popular airshow attraction and was featured in a James Bond movie. The microjet uses a TRS-18 turbojet engine and can carry only 32 gallons of fuel. Its top speed is 300 miles per hour.

fastest unmanned plane

X-43A

In November 2004, NASA launched its experimental X-43A plane for a test flight over the Pacific Ocean. The X-43A plane reached Mach 9.6, which is more than nine times the speed of sound and nearly 7,000 miles per hour. A B-52B aircraft carried the X-43A and a Pegasus rocket booster into the air, releasing them at 40,000 feet. At that point, the booster—essentially a fuel-packed engine—ignited, blasting the unmanned X-43A higher and faster, before separating from the plane. The plane continued to fly for several minutes at 110,000 feet, before crashing (intentionally) into the ocean.

largest royal caribbean cruise sister ships

Two Royal Caribbean cruise ships share the record for the largest in the world: *Oasis of the Seas* and *Allure of the Seas*. Each sister ship weighs a hefty 225,282 tons and is 1,187 feet long. Both ships feature sixteen decks with 2,700 private rooms and can carry 5,400 guests. Passengers can enjoy more than twenty restaurants, an ice-skating rink, a full-size basketball court, or a zip line nine decks up and 82 feet across. Royal Caribbean is building an even larger cruise ship, *Harmony of the Seas*, which will weigh 227,000 tons and hold 5,479 passengers.

OASIS OF THE SEAS

apollo 10
fastest manned spacecraft

NASA's *Apollo 10* spacecraft reached its top speed on its descent to Earth, hurtling through the atmosphere at 24,816 miles per hour and splashing down on May 26, 1969. The spacecraft's crew had traveled faster than anyone on Earth. The mission was a "dress rehearsal" for the first moon landing by *Apollo 11*, two months later. The *Apollo 10* spacecraft consisted of a Command and Service Module, called Charlie Brown, and a Lunar Module, called Snoopy. Today, Charlie Brown is on display at the Science Museum in London, England.

TITAN/CENTAUR

Helios 1 and Helios 2 are space probes launched in the 1970s to orbit the sun. A probe, equipped with cameras, sensors, and computers, can transmit information back to Earth. Both probes are extremely fast, with Helios 2 reaching 153,800 miles per hour. Helios 2 flew closest to the sun, getting within 32 million miles from the center of the giant star. It takes the probes about 190 days to orbit the sun. In 2018, NASA plans to send another probe, Solar Probe Plus, which will go even closer to the sun. This probe could hit speeds as high as 450,000 miles per hour.

on the move fastest roller

Fastest roller coasters

Formula Rossa, Abu Dhabi, U.A.E. **149.1 mph**

Kingda Ka, New Jersey, U.S.A. **128 mph**

Thrill seekers hurtle along the Formula Rossa track at 149.1 miles per hour. The high-speed roller coaster is part of Ferrari World in Abu Dhabi, United Arab Emirates. At 925,696 square miles, Ferrari World is the world's largest indoor theme park. The Formula Rossa roller coaster seats are red

Ferrari-shaped cars that travel from 0 to 62 miles per hour in just two seconds—as fast as a race car. The ride's G-Force is so extreme that passengers must wear goggles to protect their eyes. G-Force acts on a body due to acceleration and gravity. People can withstand 6 to 8 Gs for short periods. The Formula Rossa G-Force is 4.8 Gs during acceleration and 1.7 Gs at maximum speed.

FORMUL

coaster

Top Thrill Dragster, Ohio, U.S.A. **120 mph**

Dodonpa, Yamanashi, Japan **107 mph**

Tower of Terror II, Queensland, Australia **100 mph**

FORMULA ROSSA WORLD RECORDS
SPEED: 149.1MPH
G-FORCE: 1.7 Gs
ACCELERATION: 4.8 Gs

A ROSSA

oldest

merry-go-round

Taking a spin around the Flying Horses Carousel in Martha's Vineyard is a trip back in time. Charles Dare constructed the carousel in 1876 for an amusement park in Coney Island, New York. The carousel moved to Oak Bluffs, Massachusetts, in 1884. A preservation society took over Flying Horses in 1986 to restore the carousel and keep it intact and working. Today, the horses look just as colorful as they did in the 1800s. Their manes are real horsehair and they have glass eyes. As the horses turn around and around, a 1923 Wurlitzer Band Organ plays old-time music. The Flying Horses Carousel is a National Landmark.

flying horses
carousel

amusement park with the
most rides cedar
point

Sandusky, Ohio, is home to Cedar Point, one of the oldest continually operating amusement parks in North America. The park, which opened as a small attraction in 1870, now has seventy-two rides altogether, and many more shows and attractions. Roller coasters are a big draw. The park has seventeen thrill rides making up more than 10 miles of coaster track, including the Top Thrill Dragster, one of the world's fastest and tallest roller coasters. GateKeeper is the longest, tallest, and fastest wing roller coaster in the world. In a wing roller coaster, riders sit on either side of the track. Cedar Point is building a new roller coaster, Valravn, and aims to break even more records in the future.

Amusement parks with the most rides
Number of rides

Cedar Point, Ohio 72

Hersheypark, Pennsylvania 70

Six Flags New England, Massachusetts 59

Six Flags Great Adventure, New Jersey 52

Six Flags Magic Mountain, California 44

largest construction machine

the bagger 293

The Bagger 293 is the biggest and heaviest land vehicle in the world. This monster machine is 310 feet tall and 722 feet long. Built in Germany, the Bagger 293 is a bucket excavator, a machine that removes materials such as clay and coal from the ground. The colossal Bagger 293 is the largest of its kind. It weighs over 31 million pounds and requires five people to operate it. The bucket wheel is over 70 feet in diameter and carries eighteen buckets, each with a capacity of 1,452 gallons. Altogether, the Bagger 293 can move over eight million cubic feet every day—enough material to fill ninety-six Olympic-size swimming pools. Today, the Bagger 293 is used in a brown coal mine near Hambach, Germany.

bertha

largest tunnel-boring machine

In July 2013, Bertha started drilling out a 2-mile-long tunnel beneath Seattle, Washington. Bertha is a tunnel-boring machine built in Japan at a cost of $80 million. She weighs 7,000 tons and, at 300 feet long, she is almost the length of a football field. The machine's massive cutting head alone is 57.5 feet in diameter and consists of a steel face and 600 cutting disks. In December 2013, Bertha stopped working. The crew dug an access pit to retrieve her cutting head for repairs. In December 2015, Bertha resumed her work. The machine's fans follow Bertha's progress on her Twitter page. At one point she had 72,000 followers.

super
structures

super
structures

Selfie central

#EiffelTower

The Eiffel Tower was the most Instagrammed building of 2015—and the most visited pay-to-enter monument in the world. It was also the most popular place to take a selfie and the fourth-most-popular Facebook location check-in. In November, the iconic structure became part of the most powerful symbol of the year when artist Jean Jullien created the #PeaceforParis illustration after the bombings in the city.

trending super structures

Insta-tower

Skyscaper built in record time

In the spring of 2015, dozens of videos appeared on YouTube, Facebook, Pinterest, Twitter, and Instagram showing a superfast skyscraper construction in China—fifty-seven stories built in just nineteen days. The time-lapse videos show the building going up in seconds. The secret to the speedy build was that 95 percent of the skyscraper was put together off-site. The 1,200 workers assembled the building by stacking prebuilt parts on top of one another.

10:07 PM

Power move

Denmark breaks world record

The UN climate change Twitter account reported Denmark's wind power record for 2015: The country produced 42 percent of its electricity from wind turbines. On one day in July 2015, the country produced 140 percent of its power needs. The world's biggest wind turbine, built in Denmark, is the Vesta V164. It is 722 feet high with three 260-foot blades. The eight-megawatt turbine can produce enough power for about 13,500 households.

Thrill seekers

Millions view extreme Dream Jumping

In April 2015, extreme athletes used the world's biggest urban zip line—multiple lines totaling 6.2 miles of rope—to jump from a platform off Dubai's 1,358-foot-high Princess Tower. The video attracted over twelve million views. Dream Jumping is a form of freefall BASE jumping using a system of ropes and pulleys.

California dreaming

Golden Gate attracts record geotags

The Golden Gate Bridge in San Francisco, California, was the world's most Instagrammed bridge in 2015, just ahead of New York's Brooklyn Bridge. The picturesque suspension bridge spans 4,200 feet across the Golden Gate strait and attracts about ten million visitors a year.

city with the most skyscrapers
in the world

Hong Kong, China, has 310 buildings that reach 500 feet or higher. Six of these buildings are 980 feet or higher. The tallest three are the International Commerce Centre (ICC) at 1,588 feet; Two International Finance Centre at 1,352 feet; and Central Plaza at 1,227 feet. Hong Kong's stunning skyline towers above Victoria Harbor. Most of its tallest buildings are on Hong Kong Island, although the other side of the harbor, Kowloon, is growing. Every night a light, laser, and sound show called "A Symphony of Lights" illuminates the sky against a backdrop of some forty of Hong Kong's skyscrapers.

hong kong

City with the most skyscrapers in the world
Number of skyscrapers at 500 feet or higher

Hong Kong, China 310

New York City, U.S.A. 240

Dubai, U.A.E. 151

Shanghai, China 129

largest sports stadium

It took over two years to build Rungrado May First Stadium, a gigantic sports venue that seats up to 150,000 people. The 197-foot-high stadium opened in 1989 on Rungra Island in North Korea's capital, Pyongyang. The stadium hosts international soccer matches on its natural grass pitch, and has other facilities such as an indoor swimming pool, training halls, and a 1,312-foot rubberized running track. The annual gymnastics and artistic festival Arirang also takes place here.

Largest sports stadiums
By capacity

Rungrado May First Stadium, North Korea **150,000**

Michigan Stadium, Michigan, U.S.A. **107,601**

Beaver Stadium, Pennsylvania, U.S.A. **107, 282**

Estadio Azteca, Mexico **105, 064**

AT&T Stadium, Texas, U.S.A. **105,000**

rungrado may first stadium

largest home in an airliner

727 boeing

Bruce Campbell's home is not that large, but it is the biggest of its kind. Campbell lives in 1,066 square feet within a grounded 727 Boeing airplane. The airplane no longer has an engine, but Campbell kept the cockpit and its original instruments. He also installed a transparent floor to make the structure of the plane visible. The retired engineer purchased the plane for $100,000 and paid for its transportation to his property in Oregon. Now trees surround the plane instead of sky. Visitors are welcome to take a tour.

largest house shaped like a
VW beetle
voglreiter
residence

Architect Markus Voglreiter turned an ordinary home in Gnigl, near Salzburg, Austria, into an attention-grabbing showpiece: a Volkswagen-Beetle-shaped house. The eco-friendly home, completed in 2003, is energy efficient and offers separate, comfortable living quarters. The car-shaped extension measures 950 square feet and is over 32 feet high. At night, two of the home's windows look like car headlights.

world's most expensive hotel

A private elevator whisks guests up to the Royal Penthouse Suite on the top floor of Hotel President Wilson in Geneva, Switzerland. A stay in this luxurious suite comes with a hefty price tag—starting at about $60,000 per night. Measuring 18,082 square feet, this is Europe's biggest suite and includes twelve bedrooms, spacious marble bathrooms, a private gym, and even a Steinway piano for guests to play. Eight floors up, the rooms have panoramic views across Lake Geneva. The hotel reserves this deluxe pad for heads of state and celebrities. It comes with maximum-security features such as bulletproof windows and doors.

Most expensive hotels

Price per night in U.S. dollars

Hotel President Wilson, Switzerland $60,000

Four Seasons Hotel, New York City, U.S.A. $45,000

The Raj Palace, Jaipur, India $43,000

Laucala Island Resort, Fiji $40,000

Grand Hyatt Cannes Hotel Martinez, France $37,500

world's first hotel made of salt palacio de sal

Hotel Palacio de Sal in Uyuni, Bolivia, is the first hotel in the world made completely out of salt. Originally built in 1998, construction began on the new Palacio de Sal hotel in 2004. The hotel overlooks the biggest salt flat in the world, Salar de Uyuni, which covers 4,086 square miles. Builders used around one million blocks of salt to create the hotel walls, floors, ceilings, and furniture. Some of the hotel's thirty rooms have igloo-shaped roofs. The salt flats lie in an area once covered by Lago Minchin, an ancient salt lake. When the lake dried up, it left salt pans, one of which was the Salar de Uyuni.

ANOTHER STRANGE PLACE TO STAY

Hotel shaped like a dog: **Dog Bark Park Inn** in Cottonwood, Idaho, where you can sleep inside a wooden beagle that measures 33 feet high and 16 feet wide.

GOING UP!

THE UPPER SECTION IS STEEL FRAMED, SO IT'S **POSSIBLE TO** MAKE IT TALLER. DURING BUILDING, ITS HEIGHT WAS **RAISED THREE TIMES.**

2,684 feet !

It can sway up to 3.9 feet!

record breaker

Laid end to end the steel used here would stretch one-quarter of the way around the world!

WORLD'S tallest BUILDING

DUBAI'S BURJ KHALIFA
WORLD RECORDS:
MOST FLOORS 160
FASTEST ELEVATORS 55 feet per second
HIGHEST VERTICAL CONCRETE PUMPING
1,972 FEET

largest freestanding building

new century global center

The New Century Global Center in Chengdu, southwestern China, is an enormous 18.9 million square feet. That's nearly three times the size of the U.S. Pentagon. Completed in 2013, the structure is 328 feet high, 1,640 feet long, and 1,312 feet deep. The multiuse building houses a 4.3-million-square-foot shopping mall, two hotels, an Olympic-size ice rink, a fourteen-screen IMAX cinema complex, and offices. It even has its own Paradise Island, a beach resort complete with artificial sun.

largest swimming pool
san alfonso del mar

San Alfonso del Mar's gigantic swimming pool stretches more than half a mile along the front of the resort in Algarrobo, Chile. The turquoise-blue saltwater lagoon spreads across 19.7 acres and holds 66 million gallons of water. Its deepest section is 115 feet, allowing for water activities that include sailing, scuba diving, and kayaking. Each building has its own private sandy beach with access to the lagoon.

San Alfonso del Mar, Chile 19.7

Ocean Dome, Japan 7.4

Dead Sea, China 7.4

Orthlieb Pool, Morocco 3.7

Hayman Pool, Australia 2.5

Largest swimming pools

Size in acres

tallest tree house

the minister's house

Minister Horace Burgess began building his tree house in 1993, and took many years erecting the towering, ten-story, 97-foot-high structure. The main support is an 80-foot-tall white oak tree, while six other trees provide reinforcement. The Minister's House, as it is known, is in a wooded area in Crossville, Tennessee, and includes a church topped by a chime tower. Thousands came to visit the amazing attraction every year, until the State Fire Marshal temporarily closed the tree house in 2012 due to fire hazards.

world's greenest city

According to GreenUptown.com, the world's greenest city in 2015 was Iceland's capital city, Reykjavik. The eco-friendly city gets 100 percent of its electricity from geothermal and hydrogen power and more than 80 percent of its primary energy—heating and transportation—from renewable sources. The city began its green movement in the early 1900s when farmers began using natural hot springs to heat their homes. Reykjavik aims to be completely fossil-fuel-free by 2050. Already, the city's transportation system is one of the greenest in the world. Its buses run on zero-emission hydrogen power.

reykjavik

Reykjavik, Iceland

Bristol, England

Portland, Oregon, U.S.A.

San Francisco, California, U.S.A.

Vancouver, Canada

Greenest cities 2015
according to GreenUptown.com

largest vertical garden

kaohsiung city

A vertical garden in Kaohsiung City, Taiwan, is the largest in the world at 27,922 square feet, almost the size of ten tennis courts! The garden, also called a "green wall," was completed in June 2015 and forms part of a fence around Cleanaway Company Ltd., a waste-disposal company. Construction took about two months and more than 100,000 plants. From afar, the panorama shows a landscape at sunset, with a bright red sun. However, green walls are not only beautiful; they help to lower pollution and CO_2 emissions.

world's largest greenhouse

The Eden Project sprawls over 32 acres of land in the countryside of Cornwall, England. Nestled in the cavity of an old clay pit mine, it's the world's largest greenhouse and has been open since 2003. Eight interlinked, transparent domes house two distinct biomes. The first is a rain-forest region and the second a Mediterranean region. Each has around one thousand plant varieties. Visitors can see a further three thousand different plants in the 20 acres of outdoor gardens. During construction, the Eden Project used a record-breaking 230 miles of scaffolding.

Country with the most greenhouses

The Netherlands: Greenhouses cover more than 25 square miles of the country's entire area.

eden project

largest sculpture cut from a single piece of stone

The Great Sphinx stands guard near three large pyramids at Giza, Egypt. No one knows exactly when the Egyptians built the sphinx or why. However, historians believe that ancient people created the gigantic sculpture about 4,500 years ago for the pharaoh Khafre. They carved the sphinx from one mass of limestone in the desert floor, creating a sculpture about 66 feet high and 240 feet long. It has the head of a pharaoh and the body of a lion. The sculpture may represent Ruti, a twin lion god from ancient myths that protected the sun god, Ra, and guarded entrances to the underworld. Sand has covered and preserved the Great Sphinx, but over many years, wind and humidity have worn parts of the soft limestone away.

LION-LIKE
WITH THE HEAD OF A MAN AND THE BODY
OF A LION

GREAT

HEIGHT
66 feet

GREAT SPHINX
WORLD RECORDS
AGE: 4,500 years (estimated)
LENGTH: **240 ft**
HEIGHT: **66 ft**

EROSION
THE ROCK HAS WORN
AWAY OVER THE YEARS

LIMESTONE
CARVED FROM ONE
SINGLE PIECE OF ROCK

SPHINX

largest tomb of a known individual qin shi huang's tomb

Emperor Qin Shi Huang ruled China from 221 B.C.E. to 207 B.C.E. He is famous for uniting China's empire. In 1974, people digging a well in the fields northeast of Xi'an, in Shaanxi province, accidentally discovered the ancient tomb. Further investigation by archaeologists revealed a burial complex over 20 square miles. A large pit contained 6,000 life-sized terra-cotta warrior figures, each one different from the next and dressed according to rank. A second and third pit contained 2,000 more figures, clay horses, some 40,000 bronze weapons, and other artifacts. Historians think that 700,000 people worked for about thirty-eight years to create this incredible mausoleum. The emperor's tomb remains sealed to preserve its contents and to protect workers from possible hazards, such as chemical poisoning from mercury in the surrounding soil.

most famous mausoleum

The Taj Mahal is a stunning white marble mausoleum in Agra, India, and a UNESCO World Heritage site. Shah Jahan employed more than 20,000 workers to build the famous structure between 1631 and 1648 in memory of his third wife, Mumtaz Mahal. Carvings and inlay work with about twenty-eight different types of precious and semiprecious stones decorate the marble and create delicate patterns on the facade. A long pool in front of the Taj Mahal reflects the beautiful tomb. The Taj Mahal attracts around three million visitors each year.

Most visited mausoleums

Number of annual visitors

Anitkabir, Turkey 5 million

Taj Mahal, India 3 million

Qin Shi Huang Mausoleum, China 2 million

Lenin's Tomb, Moscow, Russia 1.5 million

milan

More than 18,000 builders, many of them children, used about 550,000 LEGO® bricks to create a 114-foot, 11-inch tower in Milan, Italy. On June 21, 2015, a crane lifted an Italian TV celebrity to the top of the tower to place the last small brick. The challenge was part of Milan's EXPO 2015 and raised money for charity. About 50,000 people came to watch the record-breaking build.

Other structures made from LEGO® bricks

Largest working trailer built with LEGO® bricks: 7 feet tall by 12 feet long
Largest LEGO® Minecraft diorama: 184 square feet

tallest structure created from LEGO® bricks

tallest sand castle

virginia key beach

It took ninety-two hours in all for a team of twenty people to create the world's tallest sand castle at Virginia Key Beach, near Miami, Florida, in October 2015. At 45 feet, 10¼ inches, it is taller than a four-story building. The crew used 1,800 tons of sand to sculpt the castle, which features sculptures of India's Taj Mahal and Italy's Leaning Tower of Pisa, among other landmarks. Turkish Airlines commissioned the sand castle to celebrate a new flight route from Miami to Istanbul, Turkey.

chapter 5

tech

high tech

Tears of joy
Emoji becomes "word" of the year

Emojis were everywhere in 2015. There are about 1,620 emojis available on iOS 9.1—but the most-used emoji was the "face with tears of joy." It was so popular that Oxford Dictionaries announced this particular emoji its Word of the Year, marking the first time for a pictograph to claim the title.

Twitter has recently developed custom emojis for major pop culture events, such as the release of the new Star Wars movie and the Wimbledon tennis championship.

trending
high tech

Meet Caitlyn

Fastest time to reach one million Twitter followers

Caitlyn Jenner's very first tweet on June 1, 2015, set a Twitter record, earning the reality show star a mega one million followers in just four hours and three minutes. On her account, she wrote, "I'm so happy after such a long struggle to be living my true self. Welcome to the world Caitlyn. Can't wait for you to get to know her/me."

Time for an Apple

Apple Watch breaks sales records

Tech trend watchers estimate that about one million Apple Watches were sold in the first twenty-four hours after its launch in April 2015. By the end of the year, the number had climbed to about seven million watches sold.

Charity begins at home

Facebook founder announces record donation

Facebook CEO Mark Zuckerberg and his wife, Priscilla Chan, welcomed a baby daughter in November 2015. In December, Zuckerberg's open letter to his daughter,

Max, created a media storm with the announcement of the Chan Zuckerberg Initiative, in which the tech giant and his wife pledged 99 percent of their Facebook shares to charity during the course of their lifetimes.

Snapchat

Fastest-growing social media app

First launched in 2011, Snapchat now has about two hundred million daily users. Usage grew by 45 percent in the first half of 2015, making it the fastest-growing app of the year. In fact, Google's most popular "how to" search by Americans was "how to use the new Snapchat update."

high tech

most "liked" instagram photo 2015 kendall jenner

Kendall Jenner's Instagram photo, posted in July 2015, shows the model with her hair fanned out in a heart pattern. Within seconds, the "likes" started adding up, mounting to 3.2 million by the end of 2015. Jenner, a model and TV personality, has more than forty-five million followers on Instagram. Her sister Kylie also makes the list of the top five "liked" photos, and has accumulated over one billion "likes" altogether. Taylor Swift, another Instagram favorite, appears on the most "liked" list several times and has more than sixty million followers.

Most "liked" Instagram Photos 2015

In millions of "likes"

💜💜💜💜💜 **Kendall Jenner 3.2 (Dec.)**

💜💜💜💜 **Taylor Swift 2.6 (Sept.)**

💜💜💜 **Taylor Swift 2.5 (July)**

💜💜 **Kylie Jenner 2.3 (July)**

💜💜 **Beyoncé 2.3 (Aug.)**

most retweeted

ellen

photo ever

deGeneres

Ellen DeGeneres's selfie taken at the 2014 Oscars is the most retweeted photo ever. The photo, which pictures DeGeneres, Bradley Cooper, Jennifer Lawrence, and many other celebrities, has over 3.3 million retweets. In just over one hour, the post was retweeted over 1 million times. The rush of activity on Twitter crashed the social networking site for a short time. Before the Oscar selfie took over Twitter, President Obama held the record for the most retweeted photo. On November 6, 2012, the president posted an election victory photo and tweet that has been retweeted over 800,000 times.

top-grossing
mobile game app
game of war: fire age

The online gaming app *Game of War: Fire Age* made $1.4 million in 2015. Players build cities, train armies, and make alliances to outwit online opponents and gain control of a virtual kingdom. Although the game is free to download, players must pay to advance past a certain level. Much of the game's success is due to a huge advertising campaign worth approximately $40 million. Ads have featured model and actress Kate Upton and singer Mariah Carey.

Top-grossing mobile game apps 2015
In U.S. dollars

Game of War: Fire Age	1,464,000
Clash of Clans	1,142,000
Candy Crush Saga	779,000
Candy Crush Soda Saga	339,000
Madden NFL Mobile	291,000

most viewed
YouTube video
ever
"gangnam
style"

Since South Korean singer Psy released "Gangnam Style" in July 2012, views of his video on YouTube have soared to over 2.4 billion. The music video had more than 500,000 views on its first day and became the first video to reach one billion. Google, which owns YouTube, had to upgrade the data processing system when "Gangnam Style" pushed the YouTube viewing counter past its limit of 2.14 billion. In 2013, Psy's follow-up, "Gentleman," gained over 900 million views.

high tech most complicated
google doodle

ludwig van beethoven's
baptism

From December 16 through December 17, 2015, Google celebrated the 245th anniversary of Ludwig van Beethoven's baptism with a special, interactive Google Doodle. In order to play the mini game, Google visitors had to arrange sheet music in the right order to get Beethoven past obstacles and to

the concert hall. The doodle included parts of Beethoven's masterpieces *Symphony No. 5, Für Elise, Moonlight Sonata*, and *Ode to Joy*. Google first introduced the Google Doodle in 2000. Since then, the company has produced two thousand doodles for homepages around the world.

top google
search in 2015

The terrorist attacks in Paris, France, sparked over 897 million searches on Google. On November 13, 2015, gunmen and bombers hit a concert hall, a major stadium, restaurants, and bars in the city, killing 130 people and injuring hundreds more. The event prompted the most searches for "Paris" in Google's history. The most searched questions were "What happened in Paris?" and "What is 'Pray for Paris'?" A French designer created an image of the Eiffel Tower in the Peace symbol. He posted it on Twitter and Instagram at midnight and it went viral immediately.

Top Google searches 2015
By U.S. users, in millions

Paris attacks 897

Adele 439

Oscars 2015 406

Caitlyn Jenner 366

U.S. Election 2016 338

product with the most facebook fans

Soft drink giant Coca-Cola was the most popular product on Facebook in 2015 with 96 million fans. The company posts photographs, videos, and updates on its Timeline while fans can post their own photos and questions. Founded in 1886, Coca-Cola is now a multibillion-dollar company, producing 3,500 different types of beverages, including Dasani, Evian, and Minute Maid. The drinks sell in over 200 countries worldwide at a rate of 1.9 billion servings per day.

coca-cola

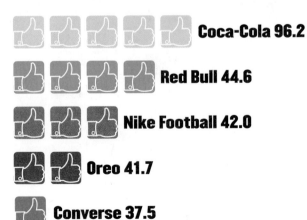

Products with the most Facebook fans
In millions

Coca-Cola 96.2

Red Bull 44.6

Nike Football 42.0

Oreo 41.7

Converse 37.5

person with the most facebook "likes"

Soccer pro Cristiano Ronaldo took the top spot on Facebook in 2015 with over 108 million fans. Born in 1985, the Portuguese player is star of the Real Madrid team in Spain. As a teenager, Ronaldo's soccer skills were so impressive that British team Manchester United signed him for around $17 million. In 2008, Ronaldo earned the honor of FIFA World Player of the Year. The following year, Ronaldo transferred to Real Madrid for a record $115 million. Among his many awards is the European Golden Shoe (formerly known as the Golden Boot), which Ronaldo has won a record four times.

cristiano ronaldo

People with the most Facebook fans
In millions

Cristiano Ronaldo 108.67

Shakira 104.19

Vin Diesel 96.66

Eminem 92.31

Lionel Messi 81.9

ATTENDANCE:
10,000 PEOPLE
73 COUNTRIES

Minecon 2015, a gathering of *Minecraft* fans, was the biggest convention ever for a single video game. The event, held July 4 to 5 in London, England, attracted 10,000 people from seventy-three countries.

Gaming developer Markus Persson created *Minecraft* in 2009 and sold it to Microsoft in 2014 for $2.5 billion. Gamers can play alone or with other players online. The game involves breaking and placing blocks to build

ON 2015

minecraft
SOLD TO
MICROSOFT FOR
$2.5 BILLION

OVER
$22 MILLION
PC/MAC GAMES
SOLD

whatever gamers can imagine—from simple constructions to huge virtual worlds. In 2014, the Ordnance Survey (O.S.) of Great Britain created the largest real-world-inspired place in *Minecraft*. Using O.S. geographical data, the creators used eighty-three billion blocks to create a map of the British Isles. At the end of 2015, *Minecraft* had sold over $22 million in PC/Mac games and had over seventy million users worldwide.

top-earning gamer 2015

peter "ppd" dager

$1,730,076.00

Top-earning eSports star Peter "ppd" Dager walked away with $1,730,076 in prize money in 2015—money won by playing video games. At 24 years old, Dager is captain of the Evil Geniuses DotA 2 (*Defense of the Ancients 2*) team, a competitive gaming group founded in 1999. Originally from Indiana, Dager now lives in California and practices for eight to ten hours a day. He also travels around the world to play in eSport tournaments, scoring a huge win—and a lot of money—at The International championship held in Seattle, Washington, in August 2015. Dager says he hopes to enroll back in school sometime to finish his communications degree.

most played online game

Every day, about 27 million online gamers battle against one another in the *League of Legends* virtual arenas. They take up almost 23 percent of online gaming time, over 16 percent more time than the next most played game, *Counter-Strike: Global Offensive*. Riot Games created *League of Legends* in 2009, and it quickly became one of the most popular MOBA—Multiplayer Online Battle Arena—games. The game is free to play, although players purchase points to buy "champions," "boosts," and other virtual items to help their chances on the battlefield.

league of legends

Most played online games 2015

Percentage of playing time on Raptr platform

🎮🎮🎮🎮🎮 *League of Legends* **22.92**

🎮🎮🎮 *Counter-Strike: Global Offensive* **6.88**

🎮🎮 *Fallout 4* **5.78**

🎮🎮 *DOTA 2* **5.09**

🎮 *World of Warcraft* **4.82**

bestselling gaming console

Sony's PlayStation 4 game console was the bestselling gaming hardware in 2015, selling 35.9 million systems worldwide. Sony sold over five million systems during the December holiday period alone. PlayStation 2 leads the world in lifetime sales, with over 157 million systems sold since its introduction in 2000. However, PlayStation 4's launch in November 2013 was the largest in history, selling over one million systems in North America within its first twenty-four hours on the market. Sony claims that the new PlayStation 4 is ten times more powerful than the older system and promises exclusive games in 2016. Diehard fans can look forward to a new survival game called *Firewatch* and *Wild*, a challenging adventure game that is set 10,000 years back in time. Both have incredible graphics. In the United States, PlayStation 4 sells for around $350, often with game bundles.

PlayStation 4

bestselling family
video game
2015

The Madden football video game franchise continued to dominate the U.S. charts in 2015. *Madden NFL 16* quickly became a fan favorite in the United States and shot to the top of the bestsellers' list. Through sophisticated graphics and animation, *NFL 16* lets gamers experience the thrill of making pro-football moves, such as bobbing and weaving through the defense to the end zone. Named after John Madden, a former NFL coach, the video game franchise started in 1988 and has grown in popularity ever since.

Top five family video games 2015

1. *Madden NFL 16*
2. *Star Wars: Battlefront*
3. *NBA 2K16*
4. *Minecraft*
5. *FIFA 16*

madden NFL 16

bestselling tech toy

sphero BB-8

© & ™ Lucasfilm Ltd.

Star Wars: The Force Awakens toys took over stores on Force Friday, September 4, 2015, with almost four thousand themed toys filling the shelves. The most popular toy was the Sphero BB-8 droid, a cute, round robot controlled with a smart phone app. On Force Friday alone, Sphero sold 2,000 BB-8s every hour, each for $150. By the end of 2015, total sales of Star Wars toys topped $700 million.

bestselling YouTube authors
dan howell and phil lester

Dan Howell and Phil Lester are British vloggers, comedians, and radio personalities whose book *The Amazing Book Is Not on Fire* shot to the top of the *New York Times* Young Adult bestseller list after its release in October 2015. It remained in the number one slot for twelve weeks. Dan Howell began his YouTube career with his channel "danisnotonfire," while Lester uploaded videos to his channel, "AmazingPhil." Each channel has millions of subscribers. The two joined forces to write their top-selling book, which is a compilation of behind-the-scenes stories, personal tales, quizzes, and photographs.

Bestselling YouTube Authors

Number of copies sold in 2015

Dan Howell and Phil Lester, *The Amazing Book Is Not on Fire* 192,600

Connor Franta, *A Work in Progress* 192,000

Tyler Oakley, *Binge* 143,500

Shane Dawson, *I Hate Myselfie* 98,900

Zoe Sugg, *Girl Online* 89,200

opportunity

longest-surviving rover on mars

Since January 2004, the Opportunity rover has been exploring planet Mars. The 384-pound NASA rover left Earth on July 7, 2003, to travel 283 million miles to Mars. Its twin rover, Spirit, left in June. The rovers, equipped with cameras and scientific equipment, landed on opposite sides of Mars and collected data on the planet's surface. NASA expected the mission to last ninety days but decided to keep the rovers on the Red Planet to explore further. NASA lost contact with Spirit in 2011, but Opportunity continues to roam Mars.

large hadron collider

largest single machine

The Large Hadron Collider (LHC) is a 16-mile, ring-shaped machine that sits 328 feet below ground on the French/Swiss border. In 2008, the European Organization for Nuclear Research (CERN) switched on the machine that thousands of scientists and engineers spent years building. They hope that the gigantic collider will explain many mysteries of the universe by examining its tiniest particles, called hadrons. The machine makes these particles travel almost at the speed of light and records what happens when they collide. The aim is to examine various scientific theories, including the idea that the universe originated in a massive cosmic explosion known as the Big Bang.

Fanny is a massive 26-foot-high, 51-foot-long, fire-breathing dragon. She is also the world's biggest walking robot. In 2012, a German company designed and built Fanny using both hydraulic and electronic parts. She is radio remote-controlled with nine controllers, while 238 sensors allow the robot to assess her environment. She does this while walking on her four legs or stretching wings that span 39 feet. Powered by a 140-horsepower diesel engine, Fanny weighs a hefty 24,250 pounds—as much as two elephants—and breathes real fire using 24 pounds of liquid gas.

FANNY
biggest walking robot

HEIGHT: 26 FEET
LENGTH: 51 FEET
WINGSPAN: 39 FEET
WEIGHT: 24,250 POUNDS

smallest robot

RoboBee

The RoboBee is smaller than a paperclip and can fly and dive into water.

Scientists and engineers at Harvard University developed the tiny robot, which has a wingspan of just over an inch and can flap its wings 120 times per second. Sensors and electronics make the bee "see" and react to its environment. Its carbon-fiber body weighs a fraction of an ounce. Initially, the lightweight robot could not break the surface of the water, so its designers lowered the wing speed to just nine beats per second. This enabled the RoboBee to get into the water and swim, but the robot cannot go back to the air. Because the RoboBee is so small, it could be useful in search-and-rescue missions and, possibly, crop pollination.

124

traxxas XO-1 supercar

fastest remote-controlled car

The Traxxas XO-1 Supercar can hit 100 miles per hour in 4.29 seconds, and reach a top speed of 118 miles per hour. The car is the fastest ready-to-race, radio-controlled car in the world. The Traxxas XO-1 comes ready to go with a brushless motor that generates 3.5 horsepower. It weighs just over 13 pounds and measures 27 inches long and almost 12 inches wide. A link app provides additional control over the radio and includes graphic data showing speed, RPM, and more. This kind of performance doesn't come cheap—even the base model Traxxas XO-1 costs as much as $750.

chapter **6**

amazing
animals

Sneaky snake
Wild animal with the most followers

A cobra escaped from New York's Bronx Zoo in 2011, but was soon returned. Safely back in his enclosure, "he" started tweeting and soon had 165,000 followers on Twitter. He tweeted his good wishes to a cobra who had escaped from the Orlando Zoo, and chastised an escaped peacock, saying: "Seriously, peacock!? We agreed we'd go tomorrow at dawn!"

trending
wild animals

RIP Cecil
Most tweeted animal

Cecil, with his distinctive black mane, was one of Zimbabwe's best-known lions. Although he lived in a national park, an American hunter first wounded him with a crossbow arrow and then, forty hours later, shot him. This happened on July 1, 2015. Animal lovers around the world were outraged—including the scientists who were studying Cecil—and he became the most tweeted animal of the year with more than 672,000 tweets on just one day.

Pizza Rat

Subway rodent video goes viral

Overnight, a hungry New York City rat became an Internet star. Comedian Matt Little uploaded a video to Instagram and YouTube of the rat dragging a slice of pizza down a subway staircase. Within twenty-four hours, the video had over two million views.

Spiky little guy

Most loved hedgehog

Newspapers all over the world recorded the passing of one little critter. He was Instagram's animal star Biddy the hedgehog, an African pygmy hedgehog, with Charlie the mini mutt as his best friend. He peaked at 598,000 followers, and would appear in different places across America extolling the virtues of the outdoor life. Biddy died on March 1, 2015, but his account is still running, "left open for everyone to enjoy."

Warning—sharks!

Twitter saves lives

In Western Australia, nearly four hundred sharks—great whites, tigers, and bronze whalers—have each been fitted with an acoustic transmitter. When one swims within a half mile of the beach, the transmitter triggers a message showing the shark's breed, size, and approximate location. This is sent out via the Twitter account of Surf Life Saving Western Australia. Not all sharks in the area are tagged, so information sent in by fishermen helps to fill in the gaps.

world's sleepiest animal

koala

Australia's koala sleeps for up to twenty hours a day, and still manages to look sleepy when awake. This is due to the koala's unbelievably monotonous diet. It feeds, mostly at night, on the aromatic leaves of eucalypt trees. The leaves have little nutritional or calorific value, so the marsupial saves energy by snoozing. It jams its rear end into a fork in the branches of its favorite tree so it cannot fall out while snoozing.

world's best glider

Flying squirrels are champion animal gliders. The Japanese giant flying squirrel has been scientifically recorded making flights of up to 164 feet from tree to tree. These creatures have been estimated to make 656-foot flights when flying downhill. The squirrel remains aloft using a special flap of skin on either side of its body, which stretches between wrist and ankle. Its fluffy tail acts as a stabilizer to keep it steady, and the squirrel changes direction by twisting its wrists and moving its limbs.

flying squirrel

World's gliders
Distance in feet

Flying squirrel 656

Flying fish 655

Colugo, or flying lemur 230

Draco flying lizard 197

Flying squid 164

african elephant

world's heaviest

The African bush elephant is the world's largest living land animal. The biggest known bush stood 13.8 feet at the shoulder and had an estimated weight of 13.5 tons. It is also the animal with the largest outer ears. The outsized flappers help to keep the animal cool on the open savanna. The Asian elephant has much smaller earflaps, because it lives in the forest and is not exposed to the same high temperatures.

land mammal

This little critter, the Kitti's hog-nosed bat, is just 1.3 inches long, with a wingspan of 6.7 inches, and weighs 0.07–0.10 ounces. It's tied for first place as world's smallest animal with Savi's pygmy shrew, which is longer at 2.1 inches but lighter at 0.04–0.06 ounces. The bat lives in West Central Thailand and southeast Myanmar, and the shrew is found from the Mediterranean to Southeast Asia.

world's tiniest bat

kitti's hog-nosed bat

world's largest primate gorilla

The largest living primates are the eastern gorillas, and the biggest subspecies is the very rare mountain gorilla. The tallest known was an adult male silverback, named for the color of the fur on his back. He stood at 6.4 feet tall, but he was an exception—silverbacks generally grow no bigger than 5.9 feet tall. Gorillas have long arms: The record holder had an arm span measuring 8.9 feet, while adult male humans have an average arm span of just 5.9 feet.

most colorful monkey in the world

mandrill

The male mandrill's face is as flamboyant as his rear end. The vivid colors of both are brightest at breeding time. The colors announce to his rivals that he is an alpha male and he has the right to breed with the females. His exceptionally long and fang-like canine teeth reinforce his dominance. As his colors fade, so does his success with the ladies. Even so, he is still the world's largest monkey, as well as the most colorful.

world's fastest
land animal
cheetah

On June 20, 2012, at the Cincinnati Zoo, a cheetah named Sarah ran the 100-meter sprint from a standing start in 5.95 seconds, beating human world-record holder Usain Bolt's 9.58 seconds. Her top speed was 61 miles per hour. In a separate time trial over a 200-meter course—this time with a running start—cheetahs reached 65 miles per hour, the highest running speed reliably timed for any animal. In the wild, with a tasty meal as the prize, these speedy animals might run even faster.

Fastest land animals
Speed in miles per hour

Cheetah 61   **African ostrich 60**   **Pronghorn 55**   **Springbok 55**   **Lion 30**

world's fastest fish

black marlin

Timing the world's
fastest fish relies on how
fast a hooked fish pulls the
line from a fisherman's reel, so
part of its escape is by swimming
and part by leaping. Using this method,
sailfish, marlin, and swordfish come out on top.
The sailfish is credited with 68 miles per hour after
fishing trials in Florida in the 1930s. A BBC film crew
claimed 80 miles per hour for a black marlin in 2001.
Then, in a computer simulation in Japan in 2008,
scientists calculated that a swordfish could reach
81 miles per hour. But this has not yet been proven
in real trials, so the black marlin stays top for now.

world's biggest big cat

Big cats are the only cats that roar. There are five of them: tiger, lion, jaguar, leopard, and snow leopard. The biggest and heaviest is the Siberian, or Amur tiger, which lives in the taiga (forestland) of eastern Siberia, where it hunts deer and wild boar. The largest reliably measured tigers have been about 11.8 feet long and weighed 705 pounds, but there have been claims for larger individuals, such as the male shot in the Sikhote-Alin Mountains in 1950. That tiger weighed 847 pounds.

world's noisiest land animal

The howler monkeys of Latin America are deafening. Males have an especially large hyoid. This horseshoe-shaped bone in the neck creates a chamber that makes the monkey's deep guttural growls sound louder for longer. It is said that their calls can be heard up to 3 miles away. Both males and females call, and they holler mainly in the morning. It is thought that these calls are often one troop telling neighboring troops where they are.

howler monkey

world's tallest living animal

giraffe

Giraffes living on the savannas of East and southern Africa are the world's tallest animals. The tallest known bull giraffe measured 19 feet from the ground to the top of his horns. He could have looked over the top of a London double-decker bus or peered into the upstairs window of a two-story house. Despite having considerably longer necks than we do, giraffes have the same number of neck vertebrae. They also have long legs with which they can either speedily escape from predators, or kick them to keep them away.

the world's largest animal . . . ever

blue whale

Blue whales are truly colossal. The largest one accurately measured was 110 feet long, and the heaviest weighed 209 tons. They feed on tiny krill, which they filter from the sea. On land, the largest known animal was a Titanosaur—a huge dinosaur that lived in what is now Argentina 101 million years ago. A skeleton found in 2014 suggests the creature was 121 feet long and weighed 77 tons. It belongs to a young Titanosaur, so an adult may have been bigger than a blue whale.

The great white shark is at the top of the list for the highest number of attacks on people. The largest reliably measured fish was 21 feet long, making it the largest predatory fish in the sea. Its jaws are lined with large, triangular, serrated teeth that can slice through flesh, sinew, and even bone. However, there were just 314 reported nonprovoked attacks between 1580 and 2014, so humans cannot be this creature's top food of choice. People don't have enough fat on their bodies. Mature white sharks prefer blubber-rich seals, dolphins, and whales. It is likely that many of the attacks on people are probably cases of mistaken identity.

GREAT WHITE SHARK

WORLD RECORDS
LENGTH: **21 FEET**

the shark most dangerous to people

GREAT WH

Shark attacks
Number of humans attacked

Great white 314

Tiger shark 111

Bull shark 100

Blacktip 29

Sand tiger 29

SHARKS HAVE
MANY ROWS OF
TEETH
GROWING IN
THEIR JAWS

ITE SHARK

whale

world's biggest fish shark

Recognizable from its spotted skin and enormous size, the whale shark is the world's largest living fish. It grows to a maximum length of about 66 feet. Like the blue whale, this mega fish feeds on some of the smallest fish: krill, marine larvae, small fish, and fish eggs. The whale shark is also a great traveler: One female was tracked swimming 4,800 miles from Mexico—where hundreds of whale sharks gather each summer to feed—to the middle of the South Atlantic Ocean, where it is thought she may have given birth.

narwhal

The narwhal's "sword" is an enormously elongated spiral tooth, or tusk. It can grow to more than 8.2 feet long. Several functions have been suggested for the tusk, from an adornment to attract the opposite sex—like a peacock's tail—to a sensory organ that detects changes in the seawater, such as saltiness, which could help the narwhal find food. Observers have noted that the larger a male narwhal's tusk, the more attractive he is to females.

world's longest tooth

world's largest crustacean

japanese spider crab

The deep-water Japanese spider crab has the largest leg span of any known crab or lobster. It comes a close second to the American lobster (the world's heaviest crustacean) by weight, and its gangly limbs can be extraordinarily long. The first European to discover this species discovered two sets of claws, measuring 10 feet long, propped up against a fisherman's hut. The crab must have been about 22 feet from one claw tip to the other when its limbs were spread apart.

world's longest
snake

The reticulated python of Indonesia is the world's longest snake. One, called Fragrant Flower, counts among the longest pythons ever discovered. It was living in the wilds of Java until villagers captured it. A local government official confirmed it was 48.8 feet long and weighed 985 pounds. These creatures are constricting snakes: They squeeze the life out of their prey. In 1999, a 22.9-foot-long python swallowed a sun bear in Balikpapan, East Kalimantan.

python

world's largest lizard komodo dragon

There are dragons on Indonesia's Komodo Island, and they're dangerous. The Komodo dragon's jaws are lined with sixty replaceable, serrated, backward-pointing teeth. Its saliva is laced with deadly bacteria and venom that the dragon works into a wound, ensuring its prey will not live for long. Prey can be as big as pigs and deer, because this lizard is the world's largest. It can grow up to 10.3 feet long and weigh 366 pounds.

world's deadliest frog

poison dart frog

A poison dart frog's skin exudes toxins. There are several species, and the more vivid a frog's color, the more deadly its poison. The skin color warns potential predators that the frogs are not good to eat, although one snake is immune to the chemicals and happily feeds on these creatures. It is thought that the frogs do not manufacture their own poisons, but obtain the chemicals from their diet of ants, millipedes, and mites. The most deadly species to people is also the largest, Colombia's golden poison dart frog. At just one inch long, a single frog has enough poison to kill ten to twenty people.

SALTWATER

world's largest reptile

The saltwater crocodile, or "saltie," is the world's
largest living reptile. Males can grow to over 20 feet
long, but a few old-timers become real monsters. A
well-known crocodile in the Segama River, Borneo, left
an impression on a sandbank that measured 33 feet.
The saltie can be found in areas from eastern India

World's largest reptiles
Length in feet

Saltwater crocodile 20

Nile crocodile 19.7

Orinoco
crocodile 19.7

Gharial 19.7

American
alligator 19

CROCODILE

to northeast Australia, where it lives in mangroves, estuaries, and rivers. It is sometimes found out at sea. It is an ambush predator, grabbing any animal that enters its domain—including people. Saltwater crocodiles account for twenty to thirty attacks on people per year, up to half of which are fatal.

world's biggest
penguin

emperor
penguin

At 4 feet tall, the emperor penguin is the world's biggest living penguin. It has a most curious lifestyle, breeding during the long, dark Antarctic winter. The female lays a single egg and carefully passes it to the male. She heads out to sea to feed, while he remains with the egg balanced on his feet and tucked under a fold of blubber-rich skin. There he stands with all the other penguin dads, huddled together to keep warm in the blizzards and 20-mile-per-hour winds that scour the icy continent. Come spring, the egg hatches, the female returns, and mom and dad swap duties, taking turns to feed and care for their fluffy chick.

World's tallest penguins
Height in inches

Emperor 48   King 39   Gentoo 35   Macaroni 28   Galapagos 19

world's smallest owl

north american elf owl

World's smallest owls
Height in inches

| North American elf owl 5 | Little owl 8.7 | Barn owl 15 | Snowy owl 28 | Great gray owl 33 |

The North American elf owl is one of three tiny owls vying for this title. It is about 5 inches long and weighs 1.5 ounces. This owl spends winter in Mexico and flies to nest in Arizona and New Mexico in spring. It often occupies cavities excavated by woodpeckers in saguaro cacti. Rivals for the title of smallest owl are Peru's long-whiskered owlet and Mexico's Tamaulipas pygmy owl, which are both a touch shorter but slightly heavier, making the elf owl the smallest of all.

hoatzin

world's smelliest bird

The hoatzin eats leaves, flowers, and fruit, and ferments the food in its crop. This habit leaves the bird with a foul odor, which has led people to nickname the hoatzin the "stinkbird." About the size of a pheasant, this bird lives in the Amazon and Orinoco river basins of South America. The hoatzin chick has sharp claws on its wings, like a pterodactyl. If threatened by a snake, the chick jumps from the nest into the water, then uses its wing claws to help it climb back up.

bird
with the
longest tail
ribbon-tailed

astrapia

The ribbon-tailed astrapia has the longest feathers in relation to body size of any wild bird. The male, which has a beautiful, iridescent blue-green head, sports a pair of white ribbon-shaped tail feathers that are more than 3.3 feet long—three times the length of its 13-inch-long body. It is one of Papua New Guinea's birds of paradise and lives in the mountain forests of central New Guinea, where males sometimes have to untangle their tails from the foliage before they can fly.

155

bird with the
longest wingspan
wandering
albatross

Long, narrow wings, like those of a glider aircraft, are the mark of the wandering albatross. The longest authenticated measurement for wingspan was taken in 1965 from an old-timer, its pure-white plumage an indication of its age. Its wingspan was 11.9 feet. This seabird rarely flaps its wings, but uses the wind and updrafts from waves to soar effortlessly over the ocean.

Birds with long wingspans
Wingspan in feet

Wandering albatross **11.9**

Great white pelican **11.81**

Andean condor **10.5**

Marabou stork **10.5**

Southern royal albatross **9.8**

bird with the
strongest forehead

The helmeted hornbill is a real bruiser. It has a structure, known as a casque, sitting atop its chisel-like bill. Unlike other hornbills, which have hollow casques, the helmeted hornbill has an almost solid one. It is filled with "hornbill ivory," which is even more valuable than elephant ivory in southern Asia. The bill and casque weigh more than 10 percent of the bird's body weight. Males use their heads as battering rams, slamming casques together in fights over territory.

helmeted
hornbill

bird that builds the largest nest

bald eagle

The world's largest nests

Diameter in inches

Bald eagle 114

White stork 57 **Golden eagle 55**

With a wingspan over 6.6 feet, bald eagles need space to land and take off—so their nests can be gargantuan. Over the years, a nest built by a pair of bald eagles in St. Petersburg, Florida, has taken on epic proportions. Measuring 9.5 feet across and 20 feet deep, it is made of sticks, grass, and moss. At one stage it was thought to have weighed at least 2 tons, making it the largest nest ever constructed by a pair of birds. Although only one pair nests at any one time, these huge structures are often the work of several pairs of birds, each building on top of the work of their predecessors.

world's largest bird egg

african ostrich egg

The African ostrich lays the largest eggs of any living bird, yet they are the smallest eggs relative to the size of the mother's body. The eggs are 5.9 inches long

4.5 in

and weigh about 3.5–5 pounds, while the mother is about 6.2 feet tall and the male 1.6 feet taller, making the ostrich the world's largest living bird. The female lays about fifty eggs per year, and each egg contains as much yolk and albumen as twenty-four hens' eggs. It takes an hour to soft boil!

5.9 in

most bees on a person

gao binggua

Bizarre as it may seem, some people cover themselves in bees . . . for fun. Chinese beekeeper Gao Binggua is one such person. In May 2015, he covered himself entirely in 1.1 million bees weighing a total of 240 pounds. First he washed himself to remove the body odors that cause bees to sting. Then he was covered with queen bees, and these attracted the workers. When they were all removed, a warm bath eased the pain of two thousand–plus bee stings!

world's fastest
flying
insect

desert
locust

Flying insects are difficult to clock, and many crazy speeds have been claimed. The fastest airspeed reliably timed was by fifteen desert locusts that managed an average of 21 miles per hour. Airspeed is the actual speed at which the insect flies. It is different from ground speed, which is often enhanced by favorable winds.

A black cutworm moth whizzed along at 70 miles per hour while riding the winds ahead of a cold front. The most shocking measurement, however, is that of a horsefly with an estimated airspeed of 90 miles per hour while chasing an air-gun pellet! The speed, understandably, has not been verified.

world's deadliest animal

Female mosquitoes live on the blood of birds and mammals—humans included. However, the problem is not what they take, but what they leave behind. In a mosquito's saliva are organisms that cause the world's most deadly illnesses, including malaria, yellow fever, dengue fever, West Nile virus, and encephalitis. It is estimated that mosquitoes transmit diseases to a staggering 700 million people every year, of which 725,000 die. Mosquitoes are the most deadly family of insects on Earth.

mosquito

world's heaviest spider
goliath bird-eating tarantula

Spiders with the largest leg spans
Span in inches

Giant huntsman spider 12

Goliath bird-eating tarantula 11

Brazilian wandering spider 5.9

Golden silk orb-weaver 5

The size of a dinner plate, the female goliath bird-eating tarantula has a leg span of 11 inches and weighs up to 6.17 ounces. This is the world's heaviest spider and a real nightmare for an arachnophobe (someone with a fear of spiders). Its fangs can pierce a person's skin, but its venom is no worse than a bee sting. The hairs on its body are more of a hazard. When threatened, it rubs its abdomen with its hind legs and releases tiny hairs that cause severe irritation to the skin. Despite its name, this spider does not actually eat birds very often.

amazing animals

Stowaway cat
Feline joyride goes viral

A small-airplane pilot in French Guiana, South America, got a shock when he spotted a cat clinging to the aircraft's wing. The pilot, Romain Jantot, landed the plane safely and the cat was unharmed. Jantot's video of the stowaway incident brought in over 18.2 million views on YouTube.

trending pet animals

Celebri-kitty
Pet with the most Facebook fans

Grumpy Cat® may be miserable, but her 8.5 million Facebook fans love her. The grouchy feline also has 1.3 million Instagram followers. Tardar Sauce, the cat's real name, is a mixed breed, born in April 2012. Her very first photo in September 2012 went viral, and she became a sensation with books, clothes, toys, and other merchandise.

Pup-tastic
Pet with the most Instagram followers

The most popular pet on Instagram is Maru, a Shiba Inu dog that lives in Japan. His owner, Shinjiro Ono, created an Instagram account in 2011 to share photos of his smiley pet. Every night, Maru says good night to his 2.4 million followers with a video or photo.

Husky mania
Most searched dog breed

The Labrador retriever may be America's most popular dog breed, but the dog with the highest number of Google searches in 2015 is the husky. Originally bred in northern Asia as a sled dog, this dog is loyal and friendly. The most searched dog-related question on Google was "Why do dogs wag their tails?"

Something to squawk about
Most searched domestic animal

The most searched animal on Google—at least by Americans—may come as a surprise: the chicken! Chickens are domestic animals, and some are kept as pets, but they were once wild. All the chickens in the Americas, Europe, and Africa are descended from the red jungle fowl of India. It is also the most common bird globally: Currently, there are more than twenty billion chickens wordwide.

world's fluffiest rabbit

In most people's opinion, the Angora rabbit is the world's fluffiest bunny. The breed originated in Turkey and is thought to be one of the world's oldest rabbits as well. It became popular with the French court in the mid-eighteenth century. Today it is bred for its long, soft, white wool, which is shorn every three to four months throughout the year. One of the fluffiest bunnies must be Ida. In 2014, she won "Best in Show" at the American Rabbit Breeders Association National Convention, the first Angora ever to do so.

angora rabbit

the world's smallest horse
thumbelina

Thumbelina is a dwarf miniature horse. At 17.5 inches tall and weighing 60 pounds, she is officially the world's smallest horse. She is stout with unusually short limbs for a horse, a far cry from the long-limbed Big Jake, the world's tallest horse: a Belgian gelding at 6.9 feet.

world's hairiest dog

komondor

The world's hairiest dog breed is the komondor, or Hungarian sheepdog. It is a powerful dog that was bred originally to guard sheep. Its long, white, dreadlock-like "cords" enable it not only to blend in with the flock, but also to protect itself from bad weather and bites from wolves. This is a large dog, standing over 27.5 inches at the shoulders. Its hairs are up to 10.6 inches long, giving it the heaviest coat of any dog.

america's most popular dog breed
labrador

The Labrador retriever has been crowned America's most popular breed for nearly one-quarter of a century. It is a gentle family companion, has an easy-to-groom coat, and needs regular exercise. Labradors were originally bred as gundogs that fetched game birds shot down by hunters. Now, aside from being a family pet, it is a favored assistance dog that helps blind people, and a good detection dog used by law-enforcement agencies.

America's most popular dogs

Rating

1 Labrador
2 German shepherd
3 Golden retriever
4 Bulldog
5 Beagle
6 Yorkshire terrier
7 Poodle
8 Boxer
9 French bulldog
10 Rottweiler

world's
tallest dog
great dane

Zeus was a Great Dane that stood 44 inches at the shoulder, making him the world's tallest dog on record. Great Danes were originally hunting dogs. They would bring down bears, boar, and deer, and pin down their quarry until the huntsman came to dispatch it. Nowadays they are known for their good nature and are considered real "gentle giants"—the world's biggest lapdogs! Sadly, Zeus died in 2014 at just five years old. There has yet to be another Great Dane tall enough to break his record.

world's

Chihuahuas are the world's smallest dog breed—and the smallest of them all is Miracle Milly, a Chihuahua from Puerto Rico. She measures just 3.8 inches tall, no bigger than a sneaker. The shortest is Heaven Sent Brandy from Florida, just 6 inches from her nose to the tip of her tail. Chihuahuas originated in Mexico, and may have predated the Maya. They are probably descendants of the Techichi, an early companion dog of the Toltec civilization (900–1168 C.E.).

smallest dog

chihuahua

america's most popular cat breed

exotic shorthair

In 2015, the Cat Fancier's Association announced that the exotic shorthair breed of cats had taken over from the Persian as the most popular breed in the United States. The exotic has a short, dense double coat with a thick undercoat and a large, round face like that of the cartoon cat Garfield. It is a cross between a Persian and an American shorthair, which was accepted as an official breed in 1966. The breed likes company, is calm like the Persian, and is a good mouser.

America's most popular cats
Rating

1 Exotic shorthair
2 Persian
3 Maine coon
4 Ragdoll
5 British shorthair
6 American shorthair
7 Abyssinian
8 Sphynx
9 Siamese
10 Scottish fold

world's **baldest** cat

The sphynx breed of cats is famous for its wrinkles and the lack of a normal coat, but it is not entirely hairless. Its skin is like the softest chamois leather, but it has a thin layer of down. It behaves more like a dog than a cat, greeting owners when they come home, and is friendly to strangers. The breed originated in Canada, where a black-and-white cat gave birth to a hairless kitten called Prune in 1966. Subsequent breeding gave rise to the sphynx.

sphynx

chapter 1

incredible
earth

incredible earth

Grand views

Most Instagrammed U.S. national park

The majestic Grand Canyon, which welcomes nearly five million visitors a year, was Instagram's most tagged US national park in 2015. Over one million Instagram posts featured #grandcanyon. Yosemite was a close second with almost 985,000 posts.

natural trending wonders

Earth love

Most followed noncelebrity Instagram

National Geographic's Instagram account is the most followed noncelebrity Instagram account, with 45.2 million followers. In May 2015, the company celebrated a total of one billion "likes" on its photos. By the end of the year, the most popular photos included one of a baby panda that earned 760,000 "likes" and a blood moon shot that reached over 1.1 million "likes."

natgeo ✔ FOLLOW

45.2
million followers
760,000

Volcanic giant
Most popular ski resort

Mammoth Mountain, California, is the ski resort with the greatest social media presence. By the end of 2015, it had 265,626 Facebook "likes" and 38,800 followers on Twitter. The resort is popular with skiers because of its unusually high snowfall.

Wish you were here!
Favorite Facebook check-in

Over one million people have checked in at Niagara Falls, Canada, via Facebook. It is the top outdoor check-in location of 2015. The waterfalls are not high, but they are extremely powerful. About six million cubic feet of water—the equivalent of about one million bathtubs full of water—flow over the Horseshoe Falls every minute.

Blood moon
Most tweeted natural phenomenon

On September 27, 2015, people all over the world shared tweets, photos, and videos of the very rare supermoon eclipse using #SuperMoon. During the phenomenon, when a full lunar eclipse occurs at the same time the moon is closest to Earth, the moon appears red and larger than usual. NASA covered the event with a live webcast from the Marshall Space Flight Center. The last supermoon eclipse occurred in 1982, and the next won't happen until 2033.

An unnamed bristlecone pine in the White Mountains of California is the world's oldest continually standing tree. It is 5,062 years old, beating its bristlecone rivals the Methuselah at 4,845 years old and Prometheus at 4,844 years old. Sweden is home to an even older tree, a Norway spruce (which are often used as Christmas trees) that took root about 9,550 years ago. However, this tree has not been standing continually, but is long-lived because it can clone itself. When the trunk dies, a new one grows up from the same rootstock, so in theory it could live forever.

oldest trees on earth
bristlecone pine

world's tallest tree

california redwood

A coast redwood named Hyperion is the world's tallest known living tree. It is 379.1 feet tall, and could have grown taller if a woodpecker had not hammered its top. It's growing in a remote part of the Redwood National and State Parks in Northern California, but its exact location is kept a secret for fear that too many visitors would upset its ecosystem. It is thought to be 700 to 800 years old.

California redwood, California, U.S.A. 379.1

Mountain ash, Tasmania 327.4

Coast Douglas fir, Oregon, U.S.A. 327.3

Sitka spruce, California, U.S.A. 317

Giant sequoia, California, U.S.A. 314

World's tallest trees
Height in feet

WATER LILY
WORLD RECORDS
LENGTH: (up to) 8.6 feet

The leaf of the giant Amazon water lily is up to 8.6 feet across. It has an upturned rim and a waxy, water-repellent upper surface. Underneath is a strong riblike structure that traps air between the ribs so the leaf floats easily. The ribs are also lined with sharp spines to protect them from aquatic plant eaters. The leaf is so large and so strong that it can support the weight of a child.

world's toughest leaf

AMAZON

IT CAN
SUPPORT THE
WEIGHT OF A CHILD

STRONG
RIBLIKE
STRUCTURE

WATER LILY

largest and heaviest fruit

pumpkin

The world's largest-ever fruit was a cultivated pumpkin grown by Swiss gardener Beni Meier, the first non-American giant pumpkin champion. His winning squash weighed an incredible 2,324 pounds, and Beni had to hire special transportation to take it for weighing in at the European Championship Pumpkin Weigh-off, held in Germany in October 2014. The seeds of nearly all giant pumpkins can trace their ancestry back to a species of squash that was cultivated by Canadian pumpkin breeder Howard Dill.

mushroom
death cap

Don't eat the death cap—the warning is in the name. This fungus is responsible for the most deaths by mushroom poisoning and can be found all over the world, including the United States. The mushroom's toxins damage the liver and kidneys, and it is not possible to destroy the dangerous chemicals by cooking, freezing, or drying. The Roman emperor Claudius is thought to have died from death cap poisoning in 54 C.E. He liked to eat a salad of Caesar mushrooms, an almost identical edible species, but was served up the killer fungus instead.

world's largest single flower

rafflesia

The scent of dead and decaying meat is not the usual quality sought in a flower, but the flies and beetles on the islands of Borneo and Sumatra love it. *Rafflesia* is known locally as the corpse flower, and at 3.3 feet across, it is the world's largest. It has no obvious stems, leaves, or roots because it is a parasite, and the only time anyone sees it is when it flowers. A female flower has to be fairly close to a male flower for successful pollination, and that is rare, because groups of flowers tend to be either one gender or the other. With forests on the two islands dwindling, the future for *Rafflesia* looks bleak.

deepest cave
on earth
krubera

The limestone-rich Western Caucasus in Abkhazia have some extraordinary cave systems. Among the caverns there is Krubera, the deepest known cave on Earth. Explorers have descended 7,208 feet from the cave entrance, and they suspect there is even more to explore. The cave is named for the Russian geographer Alexander Kruber, but the Ukrainian cave explorers have dubbed it "Crows' Cave" on account of the number of crows that nest around the entrance.

the largest cut

2.5 ct   **2.75 ct**   **3.00 ct**   **3.5 ct**   **4.00 ct**

diamond

golden jubilee

545.67 ct

(photos not to scale)

In 1985, South African miners chanced upon an enormous diamond. Jewel specialists worked for many years to hone it to perfection and fashioned a gem that was a staggering 545.67 carats, the largest cut diamond in the world. Pope John Paul II blessed the jewel, and the Thai royal family now owns it. For some time, the gem was known as Unnamed Brown, on account of its color. Today it goes by the name of Golden Jubilee. If the diamond had been colorless, it would have been worth over $14 million—however, it is a yellow-brown color and worth "only" about $12 million.

greatest number of geysers

There are about 1,000 geysers that erupt worldwide, and 540 of them are in Yellowstone National Park, USA. That's the greatest concentration of geysers on Earth. The most famous is Old Faithful, which spews out a cloud of steam and hot water to a maximum height of 185 feet every 44 to 125 minutes. Yellowstone's spectacular water display is due to its closeness to molten rock from Earth's mantle that rises up to the surface. One day the park could face an eruption one thousand times as powerful as that of Mount St. Helens in 1980.

Geyser fields
Number of geysers

Yellowstone, Idaho, Montana, Wyoming, U.S.A. 540

Valley of Geysers, Kamchatka, Russia 139

El Tatio, Andes, Chile 84

Orakei Korako, New Zealand 33

Hveravellir, Iceland 16

yellowstone national park

incredible earth

29,029 feet

Mount Everest's snowy peak is an unbelievable 5.5 miles above sea level. This mega mountain is located in the Himalayas, on the border between Tibet and Nepal. The mountain acquired its official name from surveyor Sir George Everest, but local people know it as Chomolungma (Tibet) and Sagarmatha (Nepal). In 1953, Sir Edmund Hillary and Sherpa Tenzing Norgay were the first to reach its summit. Now, more than 650 people per year manage to make the spectacular climb.

mount everest is Earth's tallest mountain above sea level

Himalayan mountains
Height above sea level in feet

Everest 29,029

K2 (Qogir) 28,251

Kanchenjunga 28,179

Lhotse 27,940

Makalu 27,838

world's greatest barrier reef

Australia's Great Barrier Reef is the only living thing that's clearly visible from space. It stretches along the Queensland coast for 1,400 miles, making it the largest coral reef system in the world. It's about half the size of Texas, with the outer reefs up to 155 miles from shore, forming a barrier between inshore waters and the deep Coral Sea. The reef is home to an astounding number of animals: over 600 species of corals alone, 133 species of sharks and rays, and 30 species of whales and dolphins.

World's longest barrier reefs
Length in miles

Great Barrier Reef, Australia 1,400

New Caledonia Barrier Reef, South Pacific 930

Mesoamerican Barrier Reef, Caribbean 620

Ningaloo Barrier Reef, Western Australia 162

world's largest hot desert
sahara desert

Sahara means simply "great desert," and great it is: It is the largest hot desert on the planet. It's the size of the United States and China combined, and dominates North Africa from the Atlantic Ocean in the west to the Red Sea in the east. It's extremely dry, with most of the Sahara receiving less than 0.1 inches of rain a year, and some places none at all for several years. It is stiflingly hot, up to 122°F, making it one of the hottest and driest regions in the world.

World's largest hot deserts
Size in square miles

Sahara Desert, North Africa 3.63 million

Arabian Desert, Western Asia 900,000

Great Victoria Desert, Australia 250,000

Kalahari Desert, Africa 220,000

Syrian Desert, Arabian peninsula 190,000

world's largest lake
caspian sea

Russia, Kazakhstan, Turkmenistan, Iran, and Azerbaijan border the vast Caspian Sea, the largest inland body of water on Earth. Once part of an ancient sea, the lake became landlocked between five and ten million years ago, with occasional fills of salt water as sea levels fluctuated over time. Now it has a surface area of about 149,200 square miles and is home to one of the world's most valuable fish: the beluga sturgeon, the source of beluga caviar, which costs up to $2,250 per pound.

Caspian Sea, Europe/Asia
149,200

World's largest lakes
Area in square miles

Lake Superior, North America
31,700

Lake Victoria, Africa
26,600

Lake Huron, North America
23,000

Lake Michigan, North America
22,300

world's longest river

nile river

People who study rivers cannot agree on the Nile's source—nobody knows where it actually starts. Some say the most likely source is the Kagera River in Burundi, which is the farthest headstream (a stream that is the source of a river) to flow into Lake Victoria. From the lake, the Nile proper heads north across eastern Africa for 4,132 miles to the Mediterranean. Its water is crucial to people living along its banks. They use it to irrigate precious crops, generate electricity, and, in the lower reaches, as a river highway.

World's longest rivers
Length in miles

Nile River, Africa 4,132

Amazon River, South America 4,000

Yangtze River, China 3,915

Mississippi–Missouri river system, U.S.A. 3,710

Yellow River, China 3,395

world's tallest
surf
waves

Many of the world's tallest waves occur at Nazaré, Portugal. In November 2011, this is where veteran surfer Garrett McNamara from Hawaii rode a 78-foot-high monster wave to seize the world record—then a couple of years later he broke the world record again, at the same spot. The wave was estimated to be at least 100 feet high, but the measurement still must be confirmed.

nazaré, Portugal

Nazaré, Portugal **100 (2013)**

Caledonia Star, South Atlantic
98.43 (2001)

World's tallest waves
Height in feet (year)

Lituya Bay, Alaska **98 (1958)**

Nazaré, Portugal **78 (2011)**

Draupner Oil Platform, Norway
60.7 (1995)

Strong winds

Most searched natural phenomenon

In October 2015, Hurricane Patricia threatened the Pacific coast of Mexico and became Google's most-searched weather event of 2015. It was a Category 5 hurricane with 165-mile-per-hour winds, making it the strongest hurricane to hit land along this stretch of coast. Although the event caused heavy rainfall and mudslides, Patricia weakened quickly as it reached land, and the region was not seriously affected.

weather trending

Hot! Hot! Hot!

Hottest year on record

Climate experts declared 2015 the hottest year since temperature records began. The National Oceanic and Atmospheric Administration confirmed on Twitter that the average temperature for the year was 58.6 degrees, about 1.62 degrees above the twentieth-century average. Global temperature has risen steadily since thermometer records began in 1850. In 2015, heat waves swept the Middle East, China, Australia, Russia, and parts of South America.

Ferocious fires

California wildfires light up the Internet

Wildfires were among the top-trending natural disasters in 2015. "Butte fire map" was the phrase entered most on Google, referring to the Butte wildfires that destroyed large swathes of Northern California. The fires killed six people and burned down more than five hundred homes. Along with the nearby Valley wildfires, these fires accounted for an estimated two billion dollars in damages.

Tornado of tweets

Twitter can help locate lost pets

Social media can help reunite pets with their owners, especially in areas where tornadoes have destroyed homes. Pets at the mercy of storms often bolt for safety, ending up far from their homes. The Twitter account for a company called Pets Located helps owners reunite with their pets. In Oklahoma, where there were seventy-five tornadoes in 2015, veterinary services post images of rescued pets on Facebook, along with details of where to find them. Many owners are reunited with their pets within twenty-four hours.

Warning!

Twitter updates follow natural disasters

The public uses social media more and more to get advance warning of earthquakes, hurricanes, and tsunamis. @NWS_ NTWC is a part of the US National Weather Service. It complements the service's website and the National Oceanic and Atmospheric Administration's Weather Radio, National Tsunami Warning Center, and Pacific Tsunami Warning Center. The Twitter feed warns followers if an earthquake or tsunami is possible.

coldest inhabited place on earth

Coldest places on Earth

Coldest temperature recorded on Earth: Vostok Station, Antarctica −128.6°F

Coldest inhabited place on Earth: Oymyakon, eastern Russia −96.2°F

Coldest annual mean temperature: Resolute, Canada 3.7°F

oymyakon

Extremely low air temperatures of −96.2°F in 1924 and −90°F in 1933 were recorded in the village of Oymyakon in eastern Russia, the lowest temperatures ever recorded in a permanently inhabited area. Only the Antarctic gets colder than this.

The five hundred people living in Oymyakon regularly experience temperatures below zero from September to May, with the December/January/February average falling well below −58°F. The town sits in a valley surrounded by snowy mountains.

hottest inhabited place on earth

dallol

Dallol, in Ethiopia, is close to the Equator and about 427 feet below sea level. In summer, it experiences the highest daily temperatures on Earth. Between 1960 and 1966, the average temperature in June was a staggering 116.1°F. At the time, Dallol was a mining settlement, trading in salt. Even the houses were made of blocks of salt. A few people remain, but today Dallol is considered a ghost town. Salt is still mined from the Danakil Depression surrounding the area.

ICE HOTEL

world's largest
ice sculpture

THE HOTEL
IS OPEN FROM
DECEMBER
TO APRIL

OTHER ICE HOTELS

SNOWCASTLE OF KEMI, FINLAND
HÔTEL DE GLACE, QUEBEC CITY, CANADA
BJORLI ICE LODGE, NORWAY
HOTEL OF ICE AT BALEA LAC, ROMANIA
ICE VILLAGE, SHIMUKAPPU, JAPAN

Want to sleep on a bed made of ice in subzero temperatures? That is the prospect for guests at the world's largest ice sculpture—the original Icehotel and art exhibition in Jukkasjärvi, 125 miles north of the Arctic Circle in Sweden. Here, the walls, floors, and ceilings of the sixty-five rooms are made of ice from the local Torne River and snow from the surrounding land. The beds, chairs, and tables—and even the bar and the drinks glasses standing on it—are made from ice. A neighboring ice church hosts one hundred weddings each winter. The hotel is open from December to April, after which it melts back into the wild.

most devastating
wildfire year
in the
united states
2015

The year 2015 was the most devastating on record for wildfires in the United States. More than ten million acres went up in smoke in the western half of the United States—across the states of California, Idaho, Montana, Wyoming, Nevada, New Mexico, Texas, and Alaska. While the number of blazes has gone down, the area destroyed has increased. Hotter, drier conditions and droughts make these fires hard to contain.

hurricane katrina

When Hurricane Katrina slammed into the Louisiana coast in 2005, a storm surge drove the sea almost 12.5 miles inland. New Orleans's hurricane surge protection was breached in fifty-three places, levees failed, boats and barges rammed buildings, and the city and countless neighboring communities were severely flooded. About 80 percent of New Orleans was underwater, close to 1,833 people lost their lives, and an area almost the size of the United Kingdom was devastated. The damage cost an estimated $108 billion. The US Home Security Secretary described the aftermath of the hurricane as "probably the worst catastrophe, or set of catastrophes" in the country's history.

Most destructive hurricanes in the United States
Wind speed in miles per hour

Labor Day Hurricane (1935) 185

Hurricane Andrew (1992) 177

Hurricane Katrina (2005) 175

Galveston Hurricane (1900) 145

most intense
storm to hit land
haiyan

Super Typhoon Haiyan is one of the most powerful storms ever recorded, and was the strongest-ever tropical storm to hit land. On November 8, 2013, it struck the Philippines, where it was known as Typhoon Yolanda.

Wind speeds reached 195 miles per hour and vast areas of the islands were damaged or destroyed. Around eleven million people were affected: Many were made homeless and at least 6,300 people were killed.

america's most
costly tornado
the joplin tornado

On May 22, 2011, a multiple-vortex tornado about one mile wide swept through Joplin, Missouri, killing 161 people and injuring more than one thousand others. It was the deadliest tornado in the United States since the 1947 Glazier-Higgins-Woodward tornadoes in which 181 people lost their lives. With $2.8 billion's worth of damage, the Joplin tornado was by far the costliest tornado in US history. It was registered as an EF5 category tornado—the most intense kind—with winds in excess of 200 miles per hour. It ripped houses off their foundations and lifted cars and trucks into the air.

highest tsunami in the united states

On July 9, 1958, a severe 7.8 magnitude earthquake triggered a huge rockslide into the narrow inlet of Lituya Bay, Alaska. The sudden displacement of water caused a mega tsunami, with a crest estimated to be 98 feet high. The giant wave traveled across the bay and destroyed vegetation up to 1,722 feet above sea level. Five people died and nearby settlements, docks, and boats were badly damaged. It was the highest tsunami to be recorded in the United States in modern times.

lituya bay
alaska

most snowfall in the united states california and colorado

The most snowfall on record in the United States overall occurred at Tamarack, near the Bear Valley ski resort in California, on March 11, 1911. The snow was an incredible 37.8 feet high. Tamarack also holds the record for the most snowfall in a month, with 32.5 feet in January 1911. Mount Shasta, California, had the most snowfall in a single storm with 15.75 feet falling from February 13–19, 1959. The most snow in twenty-four hours was a snowfall of 6.3 feet at Silver Lake, Colorado, on April 14–15, 1921.

world's largest hailstone vivian

south dakota

In August 2010, the town of Vivian, South Dakota, was bombarded by some of the biggest hailstones ever to have fallen out of the sky. They went straight through roofs of houses, smashed car windshields, and stripped vegetation. Among them was a world record breaker, a hailstone the size of a volleyball. It was 8 inches in diameter and weighed 2.2 pounds.

the human

lightning conductor

Roy Sullivan was a U.S. park ranger in Shenandoah National Park, Virginia. While going about his duties he was struck by lightning no fewer than seven times. He claimed he was also hit by lightning as a child, making a total of eight lightning strikes. It came to the point that when a thunderstorm was heard in the distance, his coworkers deliberately distanced themselves from him—just in case!

roy sullivan

chapter

8

state
stats

Snowed under

Record storm Jonas hits US East Coast

A widespread blizzard hit the East Coast on January 22–23, 2016, leading to record-breaking snowfall—and loads of memes. Dubbed "Jonas," some of the more popular memes featured musicians Joe, Kevin, and Nick Jonas, formerly of the Jonas Brothers. Baltimore, Maryland, had 29.2 inches of snow and Harrisburg, Pennsylvania, had 30.2 inches—both set new records.

states trending

Llamas on the loose

Arizona runaway llamas cause media storm

For about an hour in February 2015, two llamas ran loose in Sun City, Arizona. "Llama drama" caused a media frenzy as #llamas began trending online immediately. The two animals were eventually lassoed and taken back to their pen in Glendale.

#LoveWins

Most retweeted presidential message

On June 26, 2015, the US Supreme Court ruled in favor of gay marriage across all fifty US states. Immediately, President Obama tweeted, "Today is a big step in our march toward equality. Gay and lesbian couples now have the right to marry, just like anyone else. #LoveWins." During the next four hours, there were over 6.2 million tweets about the ruling. The hashtag #LoveWins went viral and became one of the top ten hashtags of the year.

America's pastime

Most Instagrammed stadium

Dodger Stadium was the most Instagrammed sports venue in the world in 2015. The beloved stadium in Los Angeles, California, is also the fifth most Instagrammed place in the world, beating Rome's Colosseum and Venice's Piazza San Marco. Over 147 million people have visited Dodger Stadium since it opened in 1962.

Wonderful world of Disney

Most Instagrammed place in the world

Disneyland in California was the most photographed place on Instagram in 2015. The beloved tourist destination has its own Instagram account with 2.9 million followers. Disneyland claims to have had over 650 million guests since it opened in 1955—more than any other theme park in the world.

alabama

state with the oldest mardi gras celebration

French settlers held the first American Mardi Gras in Mobile, Alabama, in 1703. Yearly celebrations continued until the Civil War and began again in 1866. Today 800,000 people gather in the city during the vibrant two-week festival. Dozens of parades with colorful floats and marching bands wind through the streets each day. Partygoers attend masked balls and other lively events sponsored by the city's social societies. On Mardi Gras, which means "Fat Tuesday" in French, six parades continue the party until the stroke of midnight, which marks the end of the year's festivities and the beginning of Lent.

state with the largest national forest

alaska

Of the 155 national forests in the United States, Tongass National Forest in southeast Alaska is by far the largest. It covers 16,800,000 acres, which is almost the size of the state of West Virginia. It is also the largest temperate rain forest in the northern hemisphere. The Tlingit and Tsimshian tribes have lived among the bears and wolves that roam Tongass for more than 10,000 years.

Two thousand bald eagles gather here each spring and thousands of snow geese stop in Tongass on their annual migration to Siberia.

Largest national forests in the United States
Size in millions of acres

Tongass National Forest, Alaska 16.8

Humboldt-Toiyabe National Forest, California/Nevada 6.3

Chugach National Forest, Alaska 5.4

Tonto National Forest, Arizona 2.8

Boise National Forest, Idaho 2.6

Kitt Peak National Observatory, 6,875 feet high in the Sonora Desert, holds the world's largest collection of optical telescopes. In addition to the twenty-five optical instruments, there are two radio telescopes and one solar telescope. Radio telescopes detect radio waves in the sky, which come from natural space objects and from man-made satellites. Scientists from around the world use the impressive McMath-Pierce Solar Telescope to study the Sun. Astronomers chose the Kitt Peak site for its relatively low levels of humidity, clear weather, and steady atmosphere, all of which allow better views into space. The observatory dates back to 1958, when the National Science Foundation leased the land from the Tohono O'odham Nation. Today, the National Optical Astronomy Observatory oversees Kitt Peak, while eight different astronomical research institutions operate and maintain the telescopes.

state that grows the most rice

arkansas

Arkansas farmers have been leading the way in rice production since the early 1900s. In 2014, the state's 2,500 rice farms collectively produced 5.6 million tons of the starchy grain—more than 50 percent of the nation's total. The average person in the United States consumes about 25 pounds of rice per year. The rice crops grow on about 1.48 million acres of land, mostly in the Grand Prairie and Delta regions in the eastern part of the state. Some 25,000 people in Arkansas are employed in the state's rice industry.

california
state with the most
visited
national site

During 2014, a record fifteen million people visited the Golden Gate National Recreation Area in California. The recreation area, located in and around San Francisco, covers more than 80,000 acres, making it one of the world's largest urban national parks. Over 300 animal species live within the park, including bobcats, snowy plovers (a type of bird), and harbor seals. Plant life ranges from towering redwoods to wildflowers such as the California poppy. Tourist hot spots include Alcatraz, the Presidio of San Francisco, and Muir Woods National Monument.

Most-visited national sites in the United States
Annual attendance, in millions

Golden Gate National Recreation Area 15.0

Blue Ridge Parkway 13.9

Great Smoky Mountains National Park 10.0

Lincoln Memorial 7.1

George Washington Memorial Parkway 7.4

state with the tallest sand dunes

colorado

At 750 feet tall, Star Dune is the highest peak in Great Sand Dune National Park, near Mosca, Colorado. Scientists estimate that the sand dunes began forming less than 440,000 years ago. Ancient lakes once filled the valley below the Sangre de Cristo Mountains. When the lakes evaporated, they left sand behind. Wind blew the sand around the mountain passes, where it collected in the low valley floor and created sand dunes. The largest dune field is 30 square miles and contains the highest sand dunes. Today, visitors have fun sledging, sliding, or skiing down the dunes. Great Sand Dune National Park also contains forests and alpine lakes, and is home to black bears and bighorn sheep.

state stats

only state to **manufacture** **PEZ** **candy**

connecticut

The PEZ factory in Orange, Connecticut, is the only place in the United States to make the world-famous candy. In 1927, an Austrian named Eduard Haas III invented PEZ as a breath mint. The letters come from the German word for peppermint, *Pfefferminz* (PfeffErminZ).The candy came to the United States in 1952, and the company opened its American factory in 1975. Today, people in the United States consume an incredible three billion PEZ candies per year. The Visitor Center in Orange displays the largest collection of PEZ memorabilia on public display in the world, including the world's largest dispenser and PEZ motorcycle.

Swedish settlers built the nation's oldest church, Old Swedes Church, in Wilmington, Delaware, from 1698 to 1699. They added the bell tower in 1802 and a stained-glass window in the mid-1840s. Otherwise, the church is largely unchanged from its original form and still holds Sunday services. The Swedes built their church around the old burial grounds of Fort Christina, the first Swedish settlement in the United States. On some nights, the church hosts a Ghosts in the Graveyard tour of the old cemetery, which dates back to 1838. In May 2015, Old Swedes Church joined the First State National Historical Park, a network of sites that focus on Delaware's colonial history.

state with the oldest church delaware

florida
state with the most
lightning
strikes

On average, there are 1,414,284 lightning strikes a year in Florida—about 24.7 strikes per square mile. Storms occur on close to 100 days a year, making Florida the Lightning Capital of the United States. The most dangerous months are June, July, and August, with most strikes occurring between noon and 6 p.m. The Sunshine State's location between the Gulf of Mexico and the Atlantic Ocean makes it a prime breeding ground for storms. High heat, winds, and humidity create ideal conditions for lightning.

States with the most lightning strikes
Annual strikes per square mile

Florida 24.7

Louisiana 19.7

Mississippi 18.4

Alabama 16.0

Arkansas 15.2

georgia

state with the largest sports hall of fame

At 43,000 square feet, Georgia's Sports Hall of Fame honors the state's greatest sports stars and coaches. The museum includes 14,000 square feet of exhibition space and a 205-seat theater. It owns more than 3,000 artifacts and memorabilia from Georgia's professional, college, and amateur athletes. At least 1,000 of these artifacts are on display at any time. The Hall of Fame corridor features over 300 inductees, such as golf legend Bobby Jones, baseball hero Jackie Robinson, and Olympic track medalist Wyomia Tyus.

GEORGIA SPORTS HALL OF FAME

Kilauea, on the Big Island of Hawaii, is 4,190 feet above sea level. This lively volcano was formed more than 300,000 years ago, and has erupted almost continuously since 1983— one of the longest known eruptions ever. The volcano's eruption rate is a

state with the most active
volcano

massive 250,000 to 650,000 cubic yards per day. An eruption that climaxed in March 1990 had covered the village of Kalapana by the end of the summer, burying more than 100 homes, a church, and a store under 50 to 80 feet of lava. Fortunately, the lava flows so slowly that the villagers had time to evacuate unharmed.

hawaii

state with the deepest
river gorge

Hells Canyon, North America's deepest river gorge, is the work of the mighty Snake River. Stretching across 120 miles, the canyon plunges as deep as 7,913 feet below He Devil Peak. Its formation began millions of years ago with volcanic activity, movement of tectonic plates, and erosion. The Snake River wound through and eroded the rocks of rising mountains, shaping the canyon as the millennia passed. Melting glaciers, rainfall, and lake flooding added to the river's power. Today, the canyon is part of Hells Canyon National Recreation Area, which extends into Idaho in the east and Oregon in the west, on both sides of the Snake River.

state stats

state that produces the most pumpkins

Illinois

Pumpkins grow on over 20,000 acres of land in Illinois—an area about the size of Manhattan. Ninety percent grow within a 90-mile radius of Peoria. Illinois produces 80 percent of the commercial pumpkins in the United States—in 2014, that amounted to 745 million pounds of this versatile member of the squash family. Although some pumpkins become jack-o'-lanterns at Halloween, most of them are processed and canned. The town of Morton, near Peoria, calls itself the Pumpkin Capital of the World. The plant here processes over 100,000 tons each year, more than 85 percent of the world's canned pumpkin.

States that produce the most pumpkins
In millions of pounds

Illinois 745.8

California 192.2

Ohio 105.3   Pennsylvania 105

Michigan 97

only state with a santa claus post office address

indiana

In 1856, the small town of Santa Fee, Indiana, changed its name to Santa Claus because the state already had a Santa Fe. The town's post office is the only one in the world with the Santa Claus name. The town is also home to the world's oldest Santa statue. The 22-foot figure was unveiled on December 25, 1935, and dedicated "to the children of the world." Every December a group of volunteers, including Santa's Elves Inc., answers some 13,000 letters that arrive in Santa Claus.

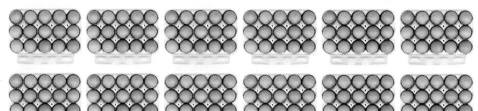

iowa

state with the highest egg production

Iowa produces nearly 16 billion eggs a year. That's enough to feed the entire nation one egg a day for forty-eight days! The state has 60 million hens, and each one lays about 279 eggs a year. These hens are hungry birds. Between them, they eat 58 million bushels of corn and 30 million bushels of soybeans a year. Americans buy 60 percent of the eggs produced, while the food service industry purchases 9 percent. Food manufacturers use the rest in food products, such as mayonnaise and cake mix.

state with the windiest city

kansas

According to data collected by the National Climatic Data Center, blustery Dodge City, Kansas, has an average wind speed of 13.9 miles per hour. Situated on the High Plains of western Kansas, Dodge City was an important stop on the old Santa Fe Trail. Founded in 1872, the city became a bustling cattle town as drivers brought herds of Texas longhorns up the Western Trail. Legendary lawmen Wyatt Earp and Bat Masterson established order in the wild and rough community. Today, Dodge City is a favorite tourist destination, drawing crowds to a string of Wild West events that take place through the year. These include the Dodge City Roundup Rodeo, a five-day event with no fewer than 800 contestants.

state with **the most** popular horse race

kentucky

The Kentucky Derby is the longest-running sporting event in the United States and proudly claims to be "the most exciting two minutes in sport." Churchill Downs racetrack in Louisville opened in May 1875, when fifteen Thoroughbreds raced in front of 10,000 cheering fans. In 2015, the race attracted a record 170,513 spectators.

Thoroughbred horses must be three years old to race the 1.25-mile-long dirt track. In 1973, Secretariat became the fastest horse ever, winning with a time of 1:59:40. The winning horse collects a cool $1 million and receives a blanket made of 554 red roses. This long-standing tradition earned the race its nickname, The Run for the Roses.

Most popular horse races in the United States
Attendance 2015

Kentucky Derby, Kentucky 170,513

Preakness, Maryland 131,680

Breeders' Cup, California 95,102

Belmont Stakes, New York 90,000

Carolina Cup, South Carolina 65,000

state with the tallest capitol building

The Louisiana State Capitol houses the state legislature and the offices of the governor and governor general. At thirty-four stories high, it looms 450 feet above the city of Baton Rouge. It is the tallest building in the city and the seventh tallest in the state. The limestone-clad building cost $5 million and took twenty-nine months to complete, finally opening in May 1932. It sits within 27 acres of landscaped grounds, which those with a head for heights can view from the observation deck on the twenty-seventh floor. Today, the building is a National Historic Landmark.

louisiana

state stats

state with the oldest state fair

MAINE

SKOWHEGAN
STATE FAIR 1880

In January 1819, the Somerset Central Agricultural Society sponsored the first-ever Skowhegan State Fair. In the 1800s, state fairs were important places for farmers to gather and learn about new agricultural methods and equipment. After Maine became a state in 1820, the fair continued to grow in size and popularity, gaining its official name in 1842. Today, the Skowhegan State Fair welcomes more than 7,000 exhibitors and 100,000 visitors. Enthusiasts can watch events that include livestock competitions, tractor pulling, a demolition derby, and much more during the ten-day show.

maryland

state with the most millionaires
per capita

A report published by an international marketing company found that almost eight of every 100 households in Maryland have $1 million in assets. Maryland gets a boost because of its proximity to Washington, DC. The states near New York City—New Jersey and Connecticut—also boast a larger than average number of millionaires for their populations. Eight of Maryland's residents made the Forbes 2015 billionaires list, including the owner of the Baltimore Ravens football team, Steve Bisciotti, whose net worth is $2.7 billion.

massachusetts
state with the oldest baseball stadium

The Boston Red Sox baseball team has been playing in its home stadium, Fenway Park, since April 20, 1912. The Sox won the World Series at Fenway that same year. Baseball legends who have played at Fenway include Babe Ruth, Jimmie Foxx, Cy Young, and Carlton Fisk. In 1946, Ted Williams hit the park's longest home run. The ball landed an amazing 502 feet from home base, and a bright red seat in the bleachers marks the spot to this day. One of Fenway's most beloved features is the Green Monster: a huge, 37-foot-high wall topped with a 23-foot-tall screen. Although it was built to keep nonpaying spectators out of the grounds, the wall is just 310 feet from home plate. This means that its height and short distance make it difficult for right-handed batters to hit home runs. The wall was covered in advertisements at first and was then painted its trademark green color in 1947. In 2003, Fenway's owners installed 269 "Monster seats" on top of the wall.

state with the largest stadium

The Big House is the affectionate nickname for Michigan Stadium, the home field of the University of Michigan Wolverines. Built in 1927 to accommodate 72,000 football fans, the stadium now seats 107,601 spectators. The original construction took 440 tons of reinforcing steel and 31,000 square feet of wire mesh. Recent additions to the Big House include luxury boxes and club seating. In 2012, Michigan Stadium hosted its first Varsity men's lacrosse match. The Varsity women's lacrosse team made their first appearance just two years later, in 2014.

michigan

GO BLUE
M CLUB SUPPORTS YOU

Largest stadiums in the United States
Seating capacity

Michigan Stadium, Michigan 107,601

Beaver Stadium, Pennsylvania 107,282

Ohio Stadium, Ohio 104,944

Kyle Field, Texas 102,512

Neyland Stadium, Tennessee 102,455

minnesota
state with the
largest indoor
amusement park

The biggest shopping mall in the United States is the Mall of America in Bloomington, Minnesota. The mall is home to Nickelodeon Universe, a 7-acre amusement park that features more than twenty rides. Rugrats Reptarmobiles, Wonder Pet's Flyboat, and Jimmy Neutron's Atomic Collider are among the favorites. Visitors can meet some of Nickelodeon's best-loved characters such as SpongeBob SquarePants and Dora the Explorer. But that's not all: The park also offers an arcade, a zipline and ropes course, and an eighteen-hole miniature golf course.

only state to hold the

international
ballet
competition

mississippi

Every four years, Jackson, Mississippi, hosts the International Ballet Competition, a two-week Olympic-style event that awards gold, silver, and bronze medals. The competition began in 1964 in Varna, Bulgaria, and rotated among the cities of Varna; Moscow, Russia; and Tokyo, Japan. In June 1979, the competition came to the United States for the first time, and, in 1982, Congress passed a Joint Resolution designating Jackson as the official home of the competition. In addition to medals, the talented dancers vie for cash prizes and the chance to join established ballet companies.

missouri

state with the largest outdoor musical theater

The Municipal Theatre in St. Louis, Missouri, opened in 1917 with a production of Verdi's opera *Aïda*. Nicknamed the Muny, the theater has a history of producing world-class operas, concerts, musicals, and ballets. Each season, the Muny presents no fewer than seven Broadway hits. Theatergoers have enjoyed such musicals as *Hairspray*, *West Side Story*, and *Beauty and the Beast*. They watch the show from one of the Muny's 10,800 flip-down seats or from one of 1,456 seats in the last nine rows that are free on a first-come-first-served basis. Set in Forest Park, the Muny's 80,000 square feet make it about the same size as a regulation-size soccer field.

Largest outdoor theaters in the United States
Area in square feet

Municipal Theatre, Missouri 80,000

Isleta Amphitheater, New Mexico 45,000

Henderson Pavilion, Nevada 40,000

Miller Outdoor Theatre, Texas 37,000

Ascend Amphitheater, Tennessee 35,000

state with the most precious sapphires

montana

Montana's nickname, The Treasure State, comes from the gold, silver, and gemstones found there. In 1879, prospectors looking for gold in Yogo Creek found bright blue pebbles in the stream. In 1894, the chief gemologist at Tiffany & Company in New York examined the pebbles and proclaimed them to be "the finest precious gemstones ever found in the United States." Yogo sapphires come only from the Yogo Gulch in the Little Belt Mountains. They are famous for their beautiful color and clarity. The British took over the mine in the late 1800s, leading to speculation that some of its stunning gems may even feature in the British Crown Jewels.

state with the largest indoor rain forest

nebraska

The Lied Jungle at Henry Doorly Zoo in Omaha, Nebraska, features three rain-forest habitats: one each from South America, Africa, and Asia. At 123,000 square feet, this indoor rain forest is larger than two football fields. It measures 80 feet high, making it as tall as an eight-story building. The Lied Jungle opened in 1992 and cost $15 million to create. Seven waterfalls rank among its spectacular features. Ninety different animal species live here, including saki monkeys, pygmy hippos, and many reptiles and birds. Exotic plant life includes the African sausage tree, the chocolate tree, and rare orchids. The zoo's other major exhibit—the Desert Dome—is the world's largest indoor desert.

nevada

The High Roller Ferris wheel in Las Vegas, Nevada, is a staggering 550 feet high, making it the tallest observation Ferris wheel in the world. The High Roller contains 7.2 million pounds of steel and never stops moving. Traveling about 10.5 inches per second, it takes thirty minutes to make a single rotation. The wheel can carry 1,120 people at once, with forty people in each of its twenty-eight pods. At night, the wheel sparkles with the help of 2,000 LED lights.

CHUTTERS
WORLD'S LONGEST CANDY COUNTER

new hampshire

state with the longest candy counter

in the world

Chutters is a candy lover's dream. The store's 112-foot-long counter houses three rows of glass jars filled with at least 500 different types of candy. Old favorites include Walnettos, Wax Bottles, Pixy Stix, and four different kinds of Bull's Eyes. Chutters is also famous for its outstanding homemade chocolate and fudge. The popular candy store, on Main Street, Littleton, began as a general store in the late nineteenth century.

new jersey

state with the world's longest boardwalk

Atlantic City's first boardwalk, built in 1870, was just 10 feet wide. After various additions and repairs, the boardwalk now stretches for 4 miles along the beach and is 60 feet wide. An adjoining boardwalk in Ventnor City extends the length to just under 6 miles. Originally, the city built the boardwalk to keep tourists from tracking sand into the beachfront hotels and railroad passenger cars. At first, there were no stores allowed near the boardwalk, but by the early 1900s, the boardwalk was one of Atlantic City's biggest attractions, lined with stores, restaurants, and the Steel Pier amusement park.

Atlantic City, New Jersey 4

Virginia Beach, Virginia 3

Coney Island, New York 2.7

Ocean City, New Jersey 2.5

Longest boardwalks in the United States
Length in miles

Wildwood, New Jersey 2

new

mexico

state with the highest
capital city elevation

Santa Fe, New Mexico, is located in the southern end of the Rocky Mountains, in the foothills of the Sangre de Cristo range. The city sits 7,000 feet above sea level. Founded in 1609–1610, Santa Fe is one of the nation's oldest capital cities and home to the oldest public building in the United States, the Palace of the Governors. Today, visitors flock to the city for its vibrant arts community, architecture, many museums, and festivals. However, it can take two days to adjust to the thin air caused by Santa Fe's high altitude.

new york

state with the most visited art museum

Each year, over six million visitors tour the Metropolitan Museum of Art in New York City. The Met, which opened on March 30, 1880, is also the largest museum in the United States, occupying 2 million square feet. The museum's collection includes two million works of art from all over the world. The American Wing alone houses 15,000 American paintings, sculptures, and articles of furniture and porcelain. Other popular exhibits at the Met include the Costume Institute and the Egyptian collection. Central to the Egyptian collection is the magnificent Temple of Dendur, relocated piece by piece from its original site near Aswan, Egypt, and housed in a glass-enclosed gallery of its own.

north carolina

state with the tallest lighthouse

Since December 1, 1870, the Cape Hatteras lighthouse has served as a beacon for ships sailing near a dangerous stretch of the Atlantic coast. Among the hazards is Diamond Shoals, a 12-mile sandbar. The lighthouse is almost 200 feet high and visitors can climb the 257 steps from the ground to the balcony level. A further twelve steps takes them up to the lantern room. Here, visitors can get an up-close look at the light, which consists of two side-by-side units facing in opposite directions. After the long climb, the metal balcony around the lantern room offers a rest and an incredible view. In 1999, beach erosion forced the National Park Service to move the lighthouse inland by 1,500 feet to its current location.

Tallest lighthouses in the United States
Height in feet

Cape Hatteras, North Carolina 200

Cape Charles, Virginia 191

Ponce de Leon, Florida 176

Absecon, New Jersey 171

Barnegat, New Jersey 171

north dakota
state with the tallest scrap metal sculpture

A spectacular sight greets travelers along Interstate 94 between Regent and Gladstone, North Dakota. Gary Greff's *Geese in Flight* is a startling 110-foot-tall, 154-foot-wide metal sculpture. Greff, who grew up in Regent, wanted to attract tourists to the area to support his hometown. *Geese in Flight* is one of seven massive art pieces along Highway 21, which is also known as the Enchanted Highway. Greff relies on fund-raising, volunteers, and donations to finance his art.

state with the most astronauts

ohio

Ohio has produced more NASA astronauts than any other state. Twenty-five astronauts were born or raised in the Buckeye State. The most prominent include Neil Armstrong, the first man to walk on the moon; John Glenn, the first American to orbit the earth; and Apollo 13 veteran Jim Lovell. Ohio astronaut Sunita Williams holds the record for total spacewalk time by a woman (fifty hours, forty minutes). NASA's Glenn Research Center is in Cleveland, Ohio.

state with the world's
largest multiple-arch dam
oklahoma

Completed in 1940, the Pensacola Dam in Oklahoma is 6,565 feet long, making it the longest multiple-arch dam in the world. The dam stretches across the Grand River and controls the 43,500 acres of water that form the Grand Lake O' the Cherokees.

The massive structure is a towering 145 feet high and consists of no fewer than 535,000 cubic yards of concrete, about 655,000 barrels of cement, 75,000 pounds of copper, and a weighty 10 million pounds of structural steel.

oregon

state with the deepest lake

Almost 7,700 years ago, Mount Mazama erupted and collapsed, creating a massive crater called a caldera. The caldera filled with rainwater and snowmelt to leave a vast lake in southern Oregon. At the depth of 1,949 feet, Crater Lake is now the deepest lake in the United States and ninth deepest in the world. Crater Lake National Park surrounds the brilliant blue lake and measures 249 square miles. The area experiences large snowfalls, with an average of 533 inches per year.

Deepest lakes in the United States
Greatest depth in feet

Lake Pend, Oreille Idaho **1,171**

Lake Superior, Michigan/ Minnesota/Wisconsin **1,330**

Lake Chelan, Washington **1,486**

Lake Tahoe, California/ Nevada **1,643**

Crater Lake, Oregon **1,949**

state that manufactures the most chocolate pennsylvania

The continental United States does not produce cocoa, but it does manufacture chocolate—and Pennsylvania is the state that makes the most. Pennsylvania is home to The Hershey Company, the country's largest chocolate manufacturer. The company controls more than 44 percent of all chocolate sales in the United States. Milton Hershey began producing milk chocolate bars and wafers in 1900 and launched the Hershey's Kiss seven years later. In 2012, the company opened a new factory in West Hershey, Pennsylvania, which can produce a mind-blowing *seventy million* Hershey's Kisses per day. The average American eats about 12 pounds of chocolate per year.

state stats

state with the oldest synagogue building

still standing in the United States

rhode island

The Touro Synagogue in Newport is the oldest synagogue building still standing in the United States. Famous self-taught architect Peter Harrison designed the synagogue in the Palladian style. The Jewish community witnessed the synagogue's dedication on December 2, 1763. It was named for Isaac Touro, the first rabbi of the congregation, whose family had come to America from Amsterdam via the West Indies. When the British captured Newport in 1776 during the American Revolution, they used the Touro Synagogue as a hospital and assembly hall. George Washington visited Newport in 1781 to meet with General Lafayette and later wrote a letter to the Touro congregation in which he stated that America would ". . . give to bigotry no sanction, to persecution no assistance."

south carolina

state with the oldest museum

In 1773, the Charleston Library founded America's first museum in Charleston, South Carolina. It opened to the public in 1824. The museum's collections include the Loeblein Gallery of Charleston Silver, natural history, Civil War artifacts, and Kidstory, a hands-on exhibit about the history of Charleston and the surrounding area. The museum also maintains two historic Charleston houses—the Heyward-Washington House, built in 1772, and the Joseph Manigault House, built in 1803.

state with the **largest wood collection**

south dakota

FREE ADMISSION
4 BLOCKS NORTH ON MAINE

The small town of Lemmon, South Dakota, is home to a 30-acre petrified wood and rock sculpture park. Locals built the park between 1930 and 1932 from petrified, or fossilized, wood and other materials found in the area. Lemmon's Petrified Wood Park exhibits include a wishing well, a waterfall, and the Castle, a 300-ton structure made from petrified wood as well as dinosaur and mammoth bones. Round "cannonball" rocks and petrified wood make up about a hundred conical "trees" in the park, some as tall as 20 feet. This intriguing park also has two museums built of petrified wood.

tennessee
state with the most species
of freshwater fish

Tennessee has 307 species of native freshwater fish living in its streams, lakes, and rivers. In addition, it has at least thirty introduced species—that is, species not native to Tennessee. Common fish types include bass, perch, and pike. The Tennessee Aquarium in Chattanooga is one of the world's largest freshwater fish aquariums. Its impressive 130,000 square feet holds 400,000 gallons of water. The Tennessee Aquarium Conservation Institute works to protect species such as Tennessee's only native trout and the 9-foot-long lake sturgeon.

States with the most species of freshwater fish

Tennessee 307

Alabama 306

Georgia 265

Kentucky 242

Virginia 217

texas: state with the most popular football team

The Dallas Cowboys scored the top spot in fan attendance records in 2014. Overall attendance was 1,209,443, with home games alone having an average of 90,069 cheering fans. The Cowboys, called America's Team, have over 8 million "likes" on Facebook and 1.4 million followers on Instagram. The Cowboys remain wildly popular, despite not winning the Super Bowl since 1996 and having three straight 8–8 seasons in a row between 2011 and 2014. Jason Garrett, head coach since 2011, is a former Dallas Cowboys player himself. The Cowboys' home stadium, AT&T Stadium, can expand to seat 100,000 fans and features an HD video board that measures 160 x 72 feet.

state with the largest
mounted
dinosaur
collection

utah

Thanksgiving Point Institute in Lehi, Utah, is a natural history museum complex. Its Museum of Ancient Life displays sixty complete, mounted dinosaur skeletons, including two massive *T. rex* specimens and a *Quetzalcoatlus* (pronounced ket-zal-koh-at-las) with an impressive 40-foot wingspan. Visitors can enjoy more than fifty hands-on exhibits, including digging for fossils and working in the Junior Paleo laboratory. The museum features the Mammoth Screen 3D Theatre, Utah's only National Geographic Experience Theater, and hosts a "Late Night with Rex" sleepover once a month.

state that produces the most maple syrup

vermont

Vermont produces almost 1.4 million gallons of maple syrup, over 40 percent of the national total. Vermont's 2,000 maple syrup producers take sap from 4.4 million tree taps. They have to collect 40 gallons of maple sap in order to produce just 1 gallon of syrup. Producers also use maple sap for making other treats, such as maple butter, sugar, and candies.

state that that has produced the most presidents

virginia

Virginia has produced eight presidents, including the nation's first, George Washington, who was born in Westmoreland County and became president in 1789. The state was the birthplace of seven more presidents, including Thomas Jefferson and Woodrow Wilson. Visitors can tour three presidential estates in Greater Charlottesville: Jefferson's Monticello, James Madison's Montpelier, and James Monroe's Ash Lawn-Highland. George Washington's estate, Mount Vernon, is in northeastern Virginia.

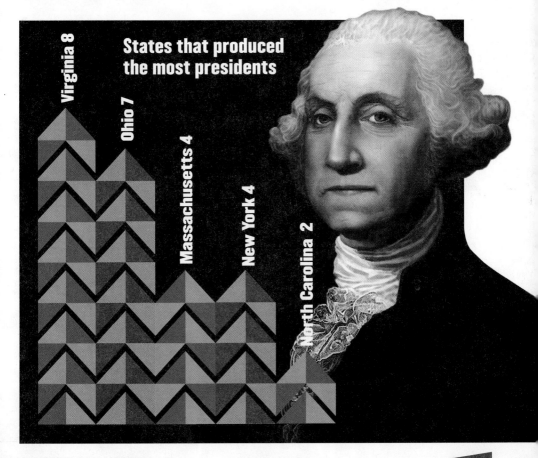

States that produced the most presidents

Virginia 8

Ohio 7

Massachusetts 4

New York 4

North Carolina 2

state with the
longest train tunnel

The Cascade Tunnel runs through the Cascade Mountains 60 miles east of Seattle. It measures 7.8 miles and is part of the main line that connects Seattle to Chicago. The Great Northern Railway began construction in 1925 to replace the original, shorter, tunnel at a higher elevation. The area's avalanches and blizzards had caused constant problems for trains. The railroad built the new, much longer Cascade Tunnel at a lower elevation, which helped ensure safer travel. However, the tunnel's length causes issues with train fumes. As a train passes through the tunnel, and for some time after, ventilation systems kick in to help remove fumes and circulate fresh air.

washington

west virginia
state with the longest
steel arch bridge

The New River Gorge Bridge in Fayetteville spans 3,030 feet and is 876 feet above the New River. It is both the longest and largest steel arch bridge in the United States. Builders used 88 million pounds of steel and concrete to construct it. The $37 million structure took three years to complete and opened on October 22, 1977. Bridge Day, held every October since 1980, is a BASE jumping event at the New River Gorge Bridge. Hundreds of BASE jumpers and some 80,000 spectators gather for the one-day festival. Among the most popular events is the Big Way, in which large groups of people jump off the bridge together. During Bridge Day 2013, Donald Cripps became one of the world's oldest BASE jumpers, at eighty-four years old.

Washington Park Velodrome in Kenosha, Wisconsin, opened in July 1927 and is the oldest operating velodrome in the nation. A velodrome is a cycling race arena with steeply banked tracks. The Kenosha Velodrome Association holds numerous races throughout the summer, but the public can use The Bowl, as it is called, on nonrace days for inline skating and running. The National Championships, held several times in Kenosha, attract thousands of spectators. In 2015, the city changed the velodrome's surface from asphalt to concrete and increased the banking at the turns.

wisconsin
state with the oldest
velodrome

state with the first national monument

Wyoming

The Devils Tower formed about sixty-five million years ago from molten lava, which cooled and eroded into hard rock. The tower rises 1,267 feet above the plains in northeastern Wyoming, overlooking the Belle Fourche River. On September 24, 1906, President Theodore Roosevelt proclaimed the landform a national monument. It was the first in the nation's history. The Plains people considered the tower a sacred site and called it Mateo Tepee, which means Grizzly Bear Lodge. When President Roosevelt declared the tower a monument, the apostrophe was left out by accident—so Devils Tower, minus the apostrophe, has remained its official name.

chapter 9

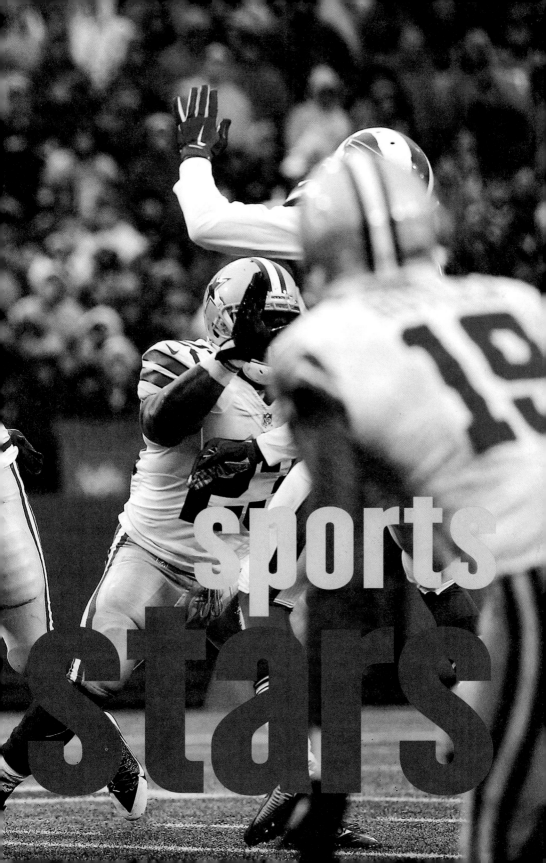

sports stars

Nike takes over

Most popular sports brand

With almost twenty-four million fans, Nike is currently the most "liked" brand on Facebook. It is also the world's most valuable sports brand, according to *Forbes* magazine. In 2015, *Forbes* calculated the brand value as $26.3 billion, around four times the second-ranked competitor in the sports market, Adidas. Nike is particularly dominant in the US basketball market, where its Air Jordan label has long been very successful.

trending sports

Real Ronaldo

Athlete with the most Instagram followers

Cristiano Ronaldo is a fan favorite on and off the soccer field. The Real Madrid superstar has a whopping 50.6 million followers on Instagram, and many of his posts have over one million "likes." Ronaldo also has over forty million Twitter followers.

Rowdy tops the charts

Most-searched female athlete

The Ultimate Fighting Championship's number one bantamweight, Ronda "Rowdy" Rousey, was the most-searched athlete and the third-most-searched person on Google in 2015. Yahoo also named Rousey as the most-searched athlete. Rousey is a mixed martial arts athlete and actress, and the UFC's first female fighter.

Golden game

Most Googled NBA team

The Golden State Warriors were the most-searched sports team on Google in 2015. The Warriors stormed into the 2015–2016 season with a record-breaking sixteen wins, the best start in NBA history. Klay Thompson also entered the history books personally in January 2015 when he scored the most points in a quarter: thirty-seven points in the third.

Score!

Soccer team tweets viewed by billions

On July 5, 2015, the United States became the first country to win three FIFA Women's World Cup titles. Tweets about the championship, tagged #FIFAWWC, were viewed nine billion times. Star player Carli Lloyd was the first player to score in four straight games, and she also scored the fastest hat trick in World Cup history. The thrilling final against Japan ended at 5–2 for the American team, making it the highest scoring game in the Cup's history.

highest BASE jump from a building

fred fugen and vince reffet

BASE jumping is just about the world's most terrifying sport to watch. BASE stands for the types of places a person may jump from: Buildings Antennae Spans (usually bridges) and Earth (usually cliffs) In April 2014, French daredevils Fred Fugen and Vince Reffet set a new record by jumping from a specially built platform at the top of the world's tallest building, the Burj Khalifa in Dubai. They jumped from a height of 2,716 feet, 6 inches. The highest ever BASE jump was performed by Russian Valery Rozov from 23,690 feet high on the north side of Mount Everest. He landed safely on the Rongbuk glacier at an altitude of 19,520 feet, some 4,100 feet below.

highest basketball shot

An Australian trick-shot team by the name of How Ridiculous is undoubtedly the champion of hitting long-range baskets. Back in 2011, the team hit a basket from a height of 219 feet, 5 inches. In June 2015, they went even farther. From the top of the Gordon Dam in Tasmania they scored a basket that was 415 feet below. That's a drop of more than 40 stories!

how ridiculous

longest
skateboard
ramp jump
danny way

Many extreme sports activities are showcased at the annual X Games and Winter X Games. At the 2004 X Games, held in Los Angeles, skateboarder Danny Way set an amazing record that remains unbeaten. On June 19, Way made a long-distance jump of 79 feet, beating his own 2003 world record (75 feet). In 2005 he jumped over the Great Wall of China. He made the jump despite having torn ligaments in his ankle during a practice jump on the previous day.

highest
tightrope walk
freddy nock

Tightrope walking looks hard enough a few feet above the ground, but Swiss stuntman Freddy Nock took it to the next level when he walked between two mountains in the Swiss Alps in March 2015. On a rope set 11,590 feet above sea level, Freddy took about thirty-nine minutes to walk the 1,140 feet across to the neighboring peak. The previous record had held since 1974, when Frenchman Philippe Petit walked between the twin towers of New York's former World Trade Center.

fastest
500-meter
speed skater

Fastest 500-meter speed skaters
Time in seconds

Pavel Kulizhnikov, Russia	33.98	2015
Jeremy Wotherspoon, Canada	34.02	2007
Lee Kang-seok, South Korea	34.25	2005
Joji Kato, Japan	34.30	2005
Hiroyasu Shimizu, Japan	34.32	2001

pavel
kulizhnikov

Following a brilliant junior skating career, Russian speedster Pavel Kulizhnikov has dominated the speed-skating scene in recent years. In two World Cup competitions in November 2015, he first broke the 500-meter world record (34.00 seconds) and then broke his own record. Kulizhnikov also won two World Championship titles earlier in 2015.

fastest
spin on ice
skates
olivia
rybicka-oliver

Although only eleven years old at the time of her record-breaking performance, Olivia Rybicka-Oliver from Nova Scotia, Canada, achieved an astonishing spin rate of 342 revolutions per minute—over five per second. This smashed the previous record of 308 revolutions per minute. Olivia, who is Polish by birth, set her record in Warsaw on January 19, 2015. Her performance was part of a fund-raising event held by Poland's Fundacja Dziecięca Fantazja (Children's Fantasy Foundation) for terminally ill children.

highest-scoring NBA game

detroit pistons

vs.

denver nuggets

1983

The Detroit Pistons and the Denver Nuggets played this game in Denver on December 13, 1983. The game went to three overtime periods before the Pistons won by 186 to 184—33 more points than the next-highest-scoring match (Spurs vs. Bucks, March 1982).

The Pistons' 186 points mark the highest total ever scored by a team. The losing team, Denver, also lost in the highest-scoring game without overtime: 162 to 158 points, won by the Golden State Warriors in November 1990.

Highest-scoring NBA games

Total points scored (final score)

Detroit Pistons vs. Denver Nuggets	370 (186–184) December 1983
San Antonio Spurs vs. Milwaukee Bucks	337 (171–166) March 1982
Golden State Warriors vs. Denver Nuggets	320 (162–158) November 1990
Denver Nuggets vs. San Antonio Spurs	318 (163–155) January 1984
Phoenix Suns vs. New Jersey Nets	318 (161–157) December 2006

NBA team
with the most
championship
titles
boston celtics

The Boston Celtics top the NBA winners' list with seventeen championship titles out of twenty-one appearances in the finals, just one title more than the Los Angeles Lakers. The two teams have met twelve times in the finals, resulting in nine wins for the Celtics. The best years for the Boston Celtics were the 1960s, with 1967 being the only year in the decade that they did not bring the championship home.

NBA championship wins		
Boston Celtics	17	1957–2008
LA Lakers	16	1949–2010
Chicago Bulls	6	1991–1998
San Antonio Spurs	5	1999–2014
Golden State Warriors	4	1947–2015

most career points in the NBA

kareem abdul-jabbar

Many fans regard Abdul-Jabbar as the greatest-ever basketball player. Before he changed his name when he converted to Islam, Abdul-Jabbar was known by his birth name, Lew Alcindor, until 1971. That same year he led the Milwaukee Bucks to the team's first NBA championship title. As well as being the all-time highest scorer of points during his professional career with a total of 38,387, Abdul-Jabbar also won the NBA Most Valuable Player (MVP) award a record six times.

NBA most career points leaders

Number of points (career years)

Kareem Abdul-Jabbar	38,387	1969–1989
Karl Malone	36,928	1985–2004
Kobe Bryant	33,182	1996–
Michael Jordan	32,292	1984–2003
Wilt Chamberlain	31,419	1959–1973

youngest player to reach 25,000 NBA career points

lebron james

Since making his NBA debut in October 2003, LeBron James has scored career points faster than any other player in pro-basketball history. He reached his latest milestone, the 25,000-point mark, on November 2, 2015, a couple of months short of his thirty-first birthday. This gives him more than three years to pass Kobe Bryant in the record for youngest to reach 30,000 points. James has been a Cleveland Cavaliers star twice, interrupted by several midcareer seasons with the Miami Heat. He has been named NBA MVP four times.

LeBron James has been the youngest player to reach every career points milestone:

1,000 points	age 19 years, 41 days	February 9, 2004
5,000 points	age 21 years, 22 days	January 21, 2006
10,000 points	age 23 years, 59 days	February 27, 2008
15,000 points	age 25 years, 79 days	March 19, 2010
20,000 points	age 28 years, 17 days	January 16, 2013
25,000 points	age 30 years, 307 days	November 2, 2015

WNBA player with the most career points

Tina Thompson was the number-one pick in the WNBA's first- ever draft in 1997. Joining the Houston Comets, she helped the team to win the championship in her rookie season. She played with the Comets until 2008 and then with the Los Angeles Sparks and Seattle Storm, before retiring in 2013. Selected nine times as a WNBA All-Star, she also won two Olympic gold medals with the U.S. national team.

Most career points in the WNBA

Number of points (career years)

Tina Thompson	7,488	1997–2013
Tamika Catchings	6,947	2002–
Diana Taurasi	6,722	2004–
Katie Smith	6,452	1999–2013
Lisa Leslie	6,263	1997–2009

tina thompson

player with the most career rebounds

lisa leslie

Most WNBA career rebounds

Number of rebounds (career years)

Lisa Leslie	3,307	1997–2009
Tamika Catchings	3,153	2002–
Tina Thompson	3,070	1997–2013
Taj McWilliams-Franklin	3,013	1999–2012
Rebekkah Brunson	2,745	2004–

Lisa Leslie joined the Los Angeles Sparks in the initial WNBA draft of 1997, after a standout college career at the University of Southern California. A 6-foot-5-inch center, she featured strongly in the lists for points and assists, as well as grabbing rebounds. She helped the Sparks to two WNBA championships and was named League MVP three times. She has won four Olympic gold medals with the U.S. national team.

women's NCAA basketball team with most championships

Connecticut

The NCAA women's basketball championship began in 1981, and two teams have dominated the competition since that time: the University of Connecticut Huskies and the Tennessee Lady Volunteers. The Huskies are currently in the lead with a tally of ten championship titles—two more than the Lady Vols have. The Huskies' great record includes the longest undefeated streak for any college basketball team, men's or women's: They won ninety games in a row, starting in 2008 and extending into 2010.

huskies

NCAA women's basketball championships

Number of titles

Connecticut Huskies	10	1995–2015
Tennessee Lady Volunteers	8	1987–2008
Louisiana Tech Lady Techsters	2	1982, 1988
Stanford Cardinal	2	1990, 1992
USC Trojans	2	1983, 1984
Baylor Lady Bears	2	2005, 2012

men's NCAA basketball team with most championships

UCLA bruins

The University of California at Los Angeles comfortably tops the list for most NCAA championships, thanks mainly to an astonishing period in the 1960s and 1970s. During this time the Bruins, inspired by their brilliant coach, John Wooden, won ten national titles in only twelve years. These wins include seven consecutive titles, from 1967 to 1973, and four undefeated seasons. The 1995 championship is the only title the Bruins have won since 1975.

dallas cowboys

NFL team most valuable

It has been twenty years since the Dallas Cowboys won the Super Bowl, yet the team has been the most valuable in the NFL for nine straight seasons up to 2015. The team was most recently valued at $4 billion. Cowboys' owner Jerry Jones paid what now seems a bargain $150 million for the franchise in 1989. In recent years broadcast and stadium revenues in the NFL have soared.

NFL team valuations

Revenue in billions of U.S. dollars
September 2015

Dallas Cowboys	$4.0
New England Patriots	$3.2
Washington Redskins	$2.9
New York Giants	$2.8
San Francisco 49ers	$2.7

NFL player with the most career touchdowns jerry rice

Jerry Rice is generally regarded as the greatest wide receiver in NFL history. He played in the NFL for twenty seasons—fifteen of them with the San Francisco 49ers—and won three Super Bowl rings. As well as leading the career touchdowns list with 208, Rice also holds the "most yards gained" mark with 22,895 yards. Most of his touchdowns were from pass receptions (197), often working with great 49ers quarterback Joe Montana.

NFL players with the most career touchdowns

Number of touchdowns (career years)

Jerry Rice	208	1985–2004
Emmitt Smith	175	1990–2004
LaDainian Tomlinson	162	2001–2011
Terrell Owens	156	1996–2010
Randy Moss	156	1998–2012

NFL player
with the most
pass
completions
brett favre

After a handful of poor games as a rookie with the Atlanta Falcons, Brett Favre moved to the Green Bay Packers, then the New York Jets and the Minnesota Vikings. He racked up twenty consecutive seasons with these teams, passing for more than 3,000 yards. Favre, also known as "The Gunslinger," beat out all other NFL players for career passes completed. He also led the Packers to victory in Super Bowl XXXI, passing for two touchdowns and scoring a third himself.

NFL players with the most pass completions

Number of completions

	Number of completions	
Brett Favre	6,300	1991–2010
Peyton Manning	6,125	1988–
Drew Brees	5,365	2001–
Dan Marino	4,967	1983–1999
Tom Brady	4,953	2000–

NFL team with the most super bowl wins

pittsburgh steelers

Although the Pittsburgh Steelers (founded in 1933 as the Pittsburgh Pirates) are one of the oldest pro-football teams, they were not very impressive in their early years. Since the 1970s, however, they have compiled one of the best all-around records in the NFL and now top the list with six Super Bowl wins out of eight appearances. The arrival of Chuck Noll as coach in 1969 was their turning point. Noll's teams, made up of such all-time greats as Terry Bradshaw, Franco Harris, and Joe Greene, won back-to-back Super Bowls twice.

NFL teams with the most Super Bowl wins

Number of wins

Team	Number of wins	Super Bowls
Pittsburgh Steelers	6	Super Bowls IX, X, XIII, XIV, XL, XLIII
San Francisco 49ers	5	Super Bowls XVI, XIX, XXIII, XXIV, XXIX
Dallas Cowboys	5	Super Bowls VI, XII, XXVII, XXVIII, XXX
Green Bay Packers	4	Super Bowls I, II, XXXI, XLV
New York Giants	4	Super Bowls XXI, XXV, XLII, XLVI
New England Patriots	4	Super Bowls XXXVI, XXXVIII, XXXIX, XLIX

fastest man in the world

usain bolt 100

Jamaica's Usain Bolt is the greatest track sprinter who has ever lived. Other brilliant Olympic finalists have described racing against him as watching him nearly disappear into the distance. Usain's greatest victories are his double Olympic gold medals at the Beijing 2008 and London 2012 games. He holds the 100-meter world record (9.58 seconds) and the 200-meter world record (19.19 seconds), both from the 2009 World Championships.

Fastest 100-meter sprints of all time

Time in seconds

Usain Bolt, Jamaica	9.58	Berlin 2009
Usain Bolt, Jamaica	9.63	London 2012
Usain Bolt, Jamaica	9.69	Beijing 2008
Tyson Gay, U.S.A.	9.69	Shanghai 2009
Yohan Blake, Jamaica	9.69	Lausanne 2012

greatest female marathon runner

paula radcliffe

British marathon runner Paula Radcliffe has held the women's marathon record since 2003, with a best time that is more than three minutes faster than anybody else's. Paula has also won World Championships in the marathon, half-marathon, and cross-country events, but, unfortunately, has never won an Olympic medal, largely due to an injury.

Fastest women's marathon times

Time in hours, minutes, and seconds

Paula Radcliffe, G.B.	2:15:25	London, 2003
Paula Radcliffe, G.B.	2:17:18	Chicago, 2002
Paula Radcliffe, G.B.	2:17:42	London, 2005
Mary Keitany, Kenya	2:18:37	London, 2012
Catherine Ndereba, Kenya	2:18:47	Chicago, 2001

LPGA golfer with the lowest seasonal average

inbee park

South Korea's Inbee Park is one of the best golfers currently playing. She has won seven major championships, with her first win in 2009 when she was only nineteen years old. Her 2015 Vare Trophy win for lowest average score (69.41) marked the second time she has held this prestigious honor (the first time being in 2012). Park came second to Lydia Ko from New Zealand in the money list in 2015, both of them winning five tournaments.

PGA golfer with the lowest seasonal average

jordan spieth

In 2015, in only his third full season as a pro, Jordan Spieth won two Majors—the Masters and the U.S. Open—and claimed a spot at the top of the world rankings. As winner of over $12 million in prize money, Spieth took virtually all the top PGA seasonal awards. He was named player of the year and won the Vardon Trophy and the Byron Nelson Award for lowest scoring average. These awards are calculated differently, but both resulted in the same score for Spieth: 68.91.

ty cobb

MLB player with the highest batting average

Highest career batting averages		
Batting averages (career years)		
Ty Cobb	.367	1905–1928
Rogers Hornsby	.358	1915–1937
Ed Delahanty	.346	1888–1903
Tris Speaker	.345	1907–1928
Ted Williams	.344	1939–1960

Ty Cobb's batting average of .367 is one of the longest-lasting records in Major League Baseball. In reaching that mark, Cobb, known to fans as "The Georgia Peach," astonishingly batted .300 or better in twenty-three consecutive seasons, mainly with the Detroit Tigers. Cobb's status in the game was made clear when he easily topped the selection poll for the first set of inductees into the Baseball Hall of Fame.

barry bonds

MLB player
with the most
home runs

Career home runs
Number of home runs (career years)

Barry Bonds	762	1986–2007
Hank Aaron	755	1954–1976
Babe Ruth	714	1914–1935
Alex Rodriguez	687	1994–
Willie Mays	660	1951–1973

Barry Bonds's power hitting and skill in the outfield rank him as a five-tool player—someone with good speed and baserunning skills, who is also good at hitting the ball, fielding, and throwing. He played his first seven seasons with the Pittsburgh Pirates before moving to the San Francisco Giants for the next twelve seasons. He not only holds the record for most career home runs, but also for the single-season record of seventy-three home runs, which was set in 2001. Barry's godfather is Willie Mays, the first player ever to hit 300 career home runs and steal 300 bases.

MLB team with the highest salary

los angeles dodgers

Unlike some other sports, Major League Baseball has no team salary cap. As team revenues from television and other sources have greatly increased in recent years, player salaries have jumped, too. For 2015, the Los Angeles Dodgers were the highest-paying club, with a player salary bill of some $273 million. This included baseball's top earner, pitcher Clayton Kershaw, who was paid a reported $34.5 million. The Dodgers won the National League West Division, but their high-earning players did not manage to progress any further in the play-offs.

MLB team with the most world series wins

new york yankees

World Series wins

Number of wins

	Number of wins		
New York Yankees	27	1923–2009	
St. Louis Cardinals	11	1926–2011	* Previously played in Kansas City and Philadelphia
Oakland Athletics*	9	1910–1989	** Previously played in New York
San Francisco Giants**	8	1905–2014	*** Originally Boston Americans
Boston Red Sox***	8	1903–2013	

The New York Yankees are far and away the most successful team in World Series history. Since baseball's championship was first contested in 1903, the Yankees have appeared forty times and won on twenty-seven occasions. The Yankees' greatest years were from the 1930s through the 1950s, when the team was led by legends like Babe Ruth and Joe DiMaggio. Nearest challengers are the St. Louis Cardinals from the National League with eleven wins from nineteen appearances.

top-earning female tennis player

serena williams

Earning more than ten million dollars in prize money alone—that is, excluding money gained through sponsorships—Serena Williams was the top-earning female tennis player of 2015.

She has been the dominant force in women's tennis in recent years, with twenty-one wins in Grand Slam singles tournaments, four Olympic gold medals, and five women's tour championships. Starting in the late 1990s, Serena's sister Venus campaigned for the Wimbledon tennis tournament to offer equal pay for male and female competitors, which it finally did in 2007. Her success means that female tennis players are now the highest-paid women in sports.

roger federer

top-earning
male tennis player

He did not win a Grand Slam title in 2015, but Switzerland's Roger Federer was comfortably the world's top-earning tennis player with a reported income of $67 million. This included some $9 million in tournament winnings. Although Novak Djokovic won almost double that, Federer was the world's top-earning performer in any sport by sponsorships, with a total of $58 million. Federer has deals with Nike and Mercedes-Benz, among others.

woman with the most grand slam titles
margaret court

The Grand Slam tournaments are the four most important tennis events of the year: the Australian Open; the French Open; Wimbledon; and the U.S. Open. The dominant force in women's tennis throughout the 1960s and into the 1970s, Australia's Margaret Court heads the all-time singles list with twenty-four, although Serena Williams is catching up fast. Court won an amazing sixty-four Grand Slam titles in singles, women's doubles, and mixed doubles, a total that seems unlikely to be beaten.

Total Grand Slam titles
Number of titles (singles titles)

Margaret Court, Australia	64 (24)	1960–1975
Martina Navratilova, Czech/U.S.A.	59 (18)	1974–2006
Billie Jean King, U.S.A.	39 (12)	1961–1980
Margaret Osborne duPont, U.S.A.	37 (6)	1941–1962
Serena Williams, U.S.A.	36 (21)	1998–2015

man with the most
grand slam singles titles
roger federer

Grand Slam singles wins		
Number of wins		
Roger Federer, Switzerland	17	2003–2012
Rafael Nadal, Spain	14	2005–2014
Pete Sampras, U.S.A.	14	1990–2002
Roy Emerson, Australia	12	1961–1967
Rod Laver, Australia	11	1960–1969
Björn Borg, Sweden	11	1974–1981

With seventeen wins between 2003 and 2012, Roger Federer stands at the top of the all-time rankings in Grand Slam tennis singles tournaments. He has achieved this despite his career overlapping with fellow greats Rafael Nadal and Novak Djokovic, who stand second and seventh in the listings. Federer's best tournament has been Wimbledon, which he has won seven times. In 2015, he was runner-up at Wimbledon and the U.S. Open.

MLS player with the most regular-season goals

landon donovan

Landon Donovan is Major League Soccer's all-time top scorer, with 144 regular-season goals (plus 28 in other matches). He also notched up 136 assists—again the record mark. In addition, Donovan holds the goal-scoring record for the U.S. national team, with 57 from 157 appearances. Donovan played for the LA Galaxy for most of his career, but also appeared and scored in the German Bundesliga and the English Premier League.

MLS regular-season top scorers
Number of goals (career years)

Landon Donovan	144	2001–2014
Jeff Cunningham	134	1998–2011
Jaime Moreno	133	1996–2010
Ante Razov	114	1996–2009
Chris Wondolowski	109	2005–

country with the most FIFA world cup wins

Brazil, host of the 2014 FIFA World Cup, has lifted the trophy the most times in the tournament's history. Second on the list, Germany, has more runners-up and semifinal appearances and hence, arguably, a stronger record overall. However, many would say that Brazil's 1970 lineup, led by the incomparable Pelé, ranks as the finest team ever. The host team has won five of the twenty tournaments that have been completed to date.

FIFA World Cup winners
Number of wins

Brazil	5	1958, 1962, 1970, 1994, 2002
Germany*	4	1954, 1974, 1990, 2014
Italy	4	1934, 1938 1982, 2006
Argentina	2	1978, 1986
Uruguay	2	1930, 1950

Three teams have won the tournament once (England 1966, France 1988, Spain 2010).

* As West Germany 1954, 1974

country with the most FIFA women's world cup wins

Fan Yunjie

Kristine Lilly

united states

Women's World Cup winners
Number of wins

United States	3	1991, 1999, 2015
Germany	2	2003, 2007
Norway	1	1995
Japan	1	2011

In 1991, the first Women's World Cup was held, in which the USA beat Norway 2–1 in the final. Since then, the United States has won the tournament twice more and has gained second or third place on every other occasion. Soccer legend Kristine Lilly was on the winning team in 1991, and again when the United States won in 1999. She competed in five World Cup tournaments total.

kristine lilly
woman with
the most
international
soccer caps

In her long and successful career, Kristine Lilly has played her club soccer principally with the Boston Breakers. When she made her debut on the U.S. national team in 1987, however, she was still in high school. Her total of 352 international caps is the world's highest for a man or woman and her trophy haul includes two World Cup winner's medals and two Olympic golds.

Women with the most international soccer caps

Number of caps (career years)

Kristine Lilly, U.S.A.	352	1987–2010
Christie Rampone, U.S.A.	311	1997–2015
Mia Hamm, U.S.A.	275	1987–2004
Julie Foudy, U.S.A.	272	1988–2004
Abby Wambach, U.S.A.	252	2001–2015

sports stars stefan everts

rider with the most motocross world titles

Winners of Motocross world titles

Number of titles

Stefan Everts, Belgium	10	1991–2006
Antonio Cairoli, Italy	8	2005–2014
Joël Robert, Belgium	6	1964–1972
Roger DeCoster, Belgium	5	1971–1976
Joël Smets, Belgium	5	1995–2003
Eric Geboers, Belgium	5	1982–1990
Georges Jobé, Belgium	5	1980–1992

As the son of Motocross World Champion Harry Everts, it is no surprise that Stefan began riding at an early age. He won his first world title in 1991, age nineteen, in the 125cc class. His final six titles (consecutive 2001–2006) were all in the premier class, latterly known as MX1. These titles were all won riding a Yamaha, but he had earlier ridden Suzuki, Kawasaki, and Honda bikes. He won fourteen of the fifteen Grand Prix races in his final season.

jockey with the most triple crown wins

eddie arcaro

Many horse-racing experts think that Eddie Arcaro was the best-ever American jockey. Arcaro rode his first winner in 1932, and by the time of his retirement thirty years later, he had won each of the three legs of the Triple Crown more times than any other jockey. Bill Hartack has since equaled Arcaro's total of five successes in the Kentucky Derby, but Arcaro is the only jockey to have completed the Triple Crown twice.

Jockeys with multiple Triple Crown wins

Number of wins

Eddie Arcaro	17	1938–1957
Bill Shoemaker	11	1955–1986
Earl Sande	9	1921–1930
Bill Hartack	9	1956–1969
Pat Day	9	1985–2000
Gary Stevens	9	1988–2013

World's top motorsport earners, 2015
In millions of U.S. dollars

Lewis Hamilton, Formula 1 — $39

Fernando Alonso, Formula 1 — $35.5

Sebastian Vettel, Formula 1 — $33

Kimi Räikkönen, Formula 1 — $27

Dale Earnhardt, Jr., NASCAR — $23.6

highest-paid
NASCAR driver
DALE EARN

Son of a NASCAR Hall of Famer, Dale Earnhardt, Jr. had his first season of top-rank NASCAR competition in 2000. His best-ever season in the drivers' competition was 2003, when he came in third, but he has been voted as the sport's most popular driver every year from then through 2015. His various sponsorship deals and business interests earned him an estimated $23.6 million in 2015. Models of his number 88 car (currently a Chevrolet SS) are the bestsellers on the market.

NHL player with the most career points

wayne gretzky

NHL all-time highest regular-season scorers

Number of points (including goals) (career years)

Wayne Gretzky	2,857 (894)	1978–1999
Mark Messier	1,887 (694)	1979–2004
Gordie Howe	1,850 (801)	1946–1979
Jaromír Jágr	1,839 (730)	1990–
Ron Francis	1,798 (549)	1981–2004

Often called "The Great One," Wayne Gretzky is regarded as the finest-ever hockey player. As well as scoring more goals and assists than any other NHL player—both in regular-season and in postseason games—Gretzky held over sixty NHL records in all by the time of his retirement in 1999. The majority of these records still stand. Although he was unusually small for an NHL player, Gretzky had great skills and an uncanny ability to be in the right place at the right time.

dave schultz

NHL player with the most penalty minutes in a season

All-time regular-season penalty minutes in the NHL

Number of minutes (career years)

Dave Williams	3,966	1974–1988
Dale Hunter	3,565	1980–1999
Tie Domi	3,515	1989–2006
Marty McSorley	3,381	1982–2001
Dave Schultz	2,294	1971–1980

Dave "The Hammer" Schultz was renowned for his aggressive style of hockey play. Born in Saskatchewan, Canada, Schultz featured in the early 1970s in a tough Philadelphia Flyers' line-up known as the "Broad Street Bullies." He racked up 472 penalty minutes in regular-season play in 1974–75—an all-time record. The Flyers won the Stanley Cup that season for the second year in succession—with Schultz adding eighty-four minutes more of penalties in postseason games!

The Canadiens are the oldest and, by far, the most successful National Hockey League team. In its earliest years, the Stanley Cup had various formats, but since 1927, it has been awarded exclusively to the champion NHL team—and the Canadiens have won it roughly one year in every four. The most successful years were the 1940s through the 1970s, when the team was inspired by all-time greats like Maurice Richard and Guy Lafleur.

montreal canadiens

NHL team with the most stanley cup wins

Stanley Cup winners (since 1915)

Number of wins

Montreal Canadiens	24	1916–1993
Toronto Maple Leafs	11	1918–1967
Detroit Red Wings	11	1936–2008
Boston Bruins	6	1929–2011
Chicago Blackhawks	6	1934–2015

highest-paid NHL player

shea weber

Star Canadian defenseman Shea Weber is reportedly set to earn $14 million in 2015–16. Weber is captain of the Nashville Predators team and has played for Nashville since he made his NHL debut in 2006. Weber has also won two Olympic gold medals with the Canada team in 2010 and 2014. However, because of the NHL's complicated salary cap rules, Weber's salary will decrease in coming seasons, and he is likely to be overtaken by, among others, Jonathan Toews and Patrick Kane, both of the Chicago Blackhawks.

Highest paid NHL players 2015–16

Salary in millions of U.S. dollars

Player	Salary	Team
Shea Weber	$14	Nashville Predators
Jonathan Toews	$13.8	Chicago Blackhawks
Patrick Kane	$13.8	Chicago Blackhawks
Sidney Crosby	$12	Pittsburgh Penguins
Henrik Lundqvist	$11	New York Rangers
Alex Ovechkin	$10	Washington Capitals

index

Photo credits

KIDS BECOME READING SUPERHEROES

The 2016 Summer Reading Challenge was one for the books! Every summer, Scholastic challenges students from around the world to read a little bit every day, just for fun. Those reading minutes add up quickly, and this year's numbers prove it! From May 9 to September 9, 2016, students from the U.S. and around the world read a whopping total of **204,594,918 minutes**! But here's the best part: Since students started logging their minutes online in 2009, they have read more than **1.2 billion minutes**—a world record in reading!

CONGRATULATIONS TO ALL STUDENTS WHO PARTICIPATED IN 2016!

STUDENTS FROM AROUND THE WORLD PARTICIPATED!

Schools from 25 countries and two U.S. territories added minutes to the Summer Reading Challenge. Five international schools each read more than **100,000 minutes**, led by Greenoak International School in Port Harcourt, Nigeria, with **1,196,525 minutes**, and Seoul Foreign School in Seoul, South Korea, with **819,079 minutes**. Top countries and territories included:

Bahamas	South Korea
Canada	Taiwan
China	Thailand
Japan	Turkey
Malaysia	Puerto Rico
Nigeria	United Arab Emirates

STATES WITH THE MOST MINUTES READ
Did your state make the top 20?

Number of participating schools:	Total number of students who logged minutes:	Number of schools logging 100,000 minutes or more:
5,154	**249,146**	**380**

STATES WITH THE MOST MINUTES READ:

1.	Texas	43,054,527
2.	Florida	18,414,561
3.	Louisiana	11,130,883
4.	Pennsylvania	10,850,122
5.	Georgia	10,147,966
6.	New York	9,021,063
7.	New Jersey	8,418,320
8.	North Carolina	7,260,459
9.	California	5,457,422
10.	Maine	5,385,682
11.	Illinois	5,172,088
12.	Michigan	4,473,354
13.	Massachusetts	4,439,854
14.	Wisconsin	3,312,368
15.	Kentucky	3,199,326
16.	Ohio	2,629,083
17.	Rhode Island	2,427,503
18.	Colorado	2,326,204
19.	Alabama	2,318,371
20.	Tennessee	2,259,166

TOP SCHOOLS IN EACH STATE!

These schools all earned top honors by reading the most in their state.

North Pole Elementary School	North Pole, AK	113,004
Williams Intermediate School	Pell City, AL	2,277,336
The New School	Fayetteville, AR	374,733
American Leadership Academy-Anthem	Florence, AZ	176,613
Hirsch Elementary School	Fremont, CA	1,117,743
Prospect Ridge Academy	Broomfield, CO	395,274
Scotland Elementary School	Scotland, CT	442,181
St. Anne's Episcopal School	Middletown, DE	110,263
Lake Nona Middle School	Orlando, FL	3,845,623
Dodgen Middle School	Marietta, GA	1,002,287
Laie Elementary School	Laie, HI	371,723
Clayton Ridge Elementary School	Guttenberg, IA	216,312
Peregrine Elementary School	Meridian, ID	1,021,856
Western Avenue Elementary School	Flossmoor, IL	379,902
St. Charles Borromeo School	Bloomington, IN	255,682
St. Thomas Aquinas School	Wichita, KS	715,842
Veterans Park Elementary School	Lexington, KY	995,118
Lisa Park Elementary School	Houma, LA	8,394,556
James M. Quinn Elementary School	North Dartmouth, MA	586,820
Fallsmead Elementary School	Rockville, MD	338,144
Brewer Community School	Brewer, ME	822,512
Daisy Brook Elementary School	Fremont, MI	810,689
Maranatha Christian Academy	Brooklyn Park, MN	470,995
Clardy Elementary School	Kansas City, MO	511,863
Annunciation Catholic School	Columbus, MS	313,131
Roosevelt Elementary School	Great Falls, MT	106,505
Etowah Elementary School	Etowah, NC	1,391,814
Erik Ramstad Middle School	Minot, ND	1,330,717
West Dodge Station Elementary School	Elkhorn, NE	463,498
Broken Ground Elementary School	Concord, NH	310,601
Newell Elementary School	Allentown, NJ	2,606,028
University Hills Elementary School	Las Cruces, NM	127,944
Double Diamond Elementary School	Reno, NV	205,616
Village Elementary School	Hilton, NY	1,164,622
McKinley Elementary School	Lisbon, OH	327,674
Northeast Elementary School	Owasso, OK	295,037
Holy Cross Catholic School	Portland, OR	247,859
Bridge Valley Elementary School	Furlong, PA	3,519,109
Robinson School	San Juan, PR	50,056
Marieville Elementary School	North Providence, RI	722,239
Varennes Academy	Anderson, SC	248,608
Castlewood Public School	Castlewood, SD	64,790
Crosswind Elementary School	Collierville, TN	773,572
Carroll Elementary School	Houston, TX	7,598,058
St. John the Baptist Elementary School	Draper, UT	433,633
Ashburn Elementary School	Ashburn, VA	1,298,048
Joseph A. Gomez Elementary School	St. Thomas, VI	3,821
Calais Elementary School	Plainfield, VT	145,644
Highlands Elementary School	Renton, WA	517,495
Hillcrest Elementary School	Chippewa Falls, WI	946,226
St. Francis Central Catholic School	Morgantown, WV	590,146
Little Snake River Valley School	Baggs, WY	149,164

MILLION MINUTE READERS CLUB!

Outside of the top 20 schools, students at these schools reached these awesome milestones.

Gray Elementary School	Houston, TX	4,193,388
New River Elementary School	Wesley Chapel, FL	2,828,918
Beacon Cove Intermediate School	Jupiter, FL	2,625,074
Raymond Academy	Houston, TX	2,119,949
Francis Elementary School	Houston, TX	2,011,364
Martin Luther King Elementary School	Edison, NJ	1,887,637
Bussey Elementary School	Houston, TX	1,721,225
Stephens Elementary School	Houston, TX	1,516,884
Combs Elementary Magnet School	Raleigh, NC	1,357,770
Kujawa Elementary School	Houston, TX	1,269,494
Ann Street School	Newark, NJ	1,207,784
Worsham Elementary School	Houston, TX	1,189,752
Ballantyne Elementary School	Charlotte, NC	1,082,900
Odom Elementary School	Houston, TX	1,063,698

THE SUMMER READING CHALLENGE GOES VIRAL!

School's out! Thousands of kids were excited about reading over the summer—and about choosing what they wanted to read! Check out these cool events, stats, and viral moments from the summer challenge!

Schools from all 50 states received books for their students to kick off summer as part of **Dav Pilkey's "Be a Reading Superhero"** Educator Contest. Iowa winner Southeast Elementary School celebrated with a parade featuring costumes, themed floats, and more!

The **Scholastic Summer Reading Road Trip** toured the country visiting communities big and small, featuring favorite authors, illustrators, and characters! The 25+ city tour included more than 50 events, visiting local bookstores, schools, and libraries across the country. Two RVs traveled a combined 10,000 miles!

The First Gentleman of Rhode Island, Andy Moffit, a **Scholastic Summer Reading Ambassador**, paid a visit to Ella Risk Elementary School.

Arizona First Lady Angela Ducey, a **Scholastic Summer Reading Ambassador**, visited Maryvale Preparatory Academy.

Staff and volunteers at Northstar Christian Academy in Rochester, NY, held a midsummer overnight **Book Camp** featuring a campout on the school grounds, s'mores, and lots of reading. Students logged **540,113 minutes** in the **Scholastic Summer Reading Challenge**!

Lisa Park Elementary School in Houma, LA, celebrated reading more than **8 million minutes**.

Students at Bridge Valley Elementary School in Furlong, PA, read more than **3.5 million minutes**!

At Carroll Elementary School in Houston, TX, students read more than **7.5 million minutes**!

North Pole Elementary School students logged the most minutes in Alaska!

Erik Ramsted Middle School students read **1,330,317 minutes** to be top in North Dakota!

Teachers at Central Elementary School in Reading, OH, celebrated winning books in **Dav Pilkey's "Be a Reading Superhero"** Contest.

Readers with the most minutes in each grade at Ashburn Elementary, Virginia's top school, celebrated with Steve Somers, the Amazing Teacher, and a bunny!